The Wealth of the World and the Poverty of Nations

The Wealth of the World and the Poverty of Nations

Daniel Cohen

translated by Jacqueline Lindenfeld

The MIT Press
Cambridge, Massachusetts
London, England

Second printing, 1998
© 1998 Massachusetts Institute of Technology

Set in Sabon by The MIT Press.
Printed and bound in the United States of America.

Library of Congress Cataloging-in-Publication Data

Cohen, Daniel, 1953–
  [Richesse du monde, pauvreté des nations. English]
  The wealth of the world and the poverty of nations / Daniel Cohen;
  translated by Jacqueline Lindenfeld.
      p.   cm.
  Includes bibliographical references and index.
  ISBN 0-262-03253-8 (hardcover : alk. paper)
    1. International economic relations.   2. Economic development.
I. Title.
HF1359.C6513   1998
337—dc21   97–38755
                                                        CIP

to the memory of Emilie

The whole idea of the sea is in any drop of water.

—Spinoza

Contents

The Wealth of the World and the Poverty of Nations

Introduction

The world is getting rich at a heretofore unknown pace. India and China, the two most populous countries, grow each year at extraordinary rates of 7 percent and 10 percent. Hong Kong and Singapore, once warehouses of the British Empire, are now wealthier than Great Britain. The world is witnessing an irreversible phenomenon resembling the "golden age" that followed World War II. On the other hand, poverty, a disease the Western countries thought they had overcome, is affecting them again. New pockets of poverty are undermining prosperity, making it look more tenuous. European unemployment and the emergence of the American "working poor" suddenly lend a bitter taste to Western wealth.

The present situation, in which poor countries are becoming richer and rich countries seem to be becoming poorer, inescapably gives credence to theories according to which the first phenomenon is responsible for the second. The sudden appearance of millions of workers from the Chinese and Indian countryside is a replay of the age-old story of the West's suffering the onslaught of Asian hordes, or perhaps of the West's attempting to resist the lure of their goods. "Every year India, China and Arabia rob our Empire of one hundred million sesterces," complained Pliny the Elder. "Such is the price of our luxury and what our women cost us, since I wonder what proportion of these goods goes to the gods of heaven and what proportion to the gods of hell."[1] These remarks, in which virtue and greed are reconciled, bear an eerie resemblance to recent statements. Today, the great fear of the West is that trade with India, with China, or with the former Soviet republics will cause the welfare state and the well-being of society to collapse.

In a few short years, "globalization" has become a loaded word both for those who advocate accepting the changes now underway and for those who would rather fight to preserve the social order so painstakingly established. Which of these apprehensions stem from myth, and which are grounded in reality? Are we to believe, literally, that trade with poor countries in itself can be blamed for our "impoverishment" when it still represents less than 3 percent of the wealth produced each year by the richest countries? Obviously, no. As I will attempt to demonstrate in this book, there is practically no foundation for the alarmist position according to which "globalization" is to be blamed for the crises currently experienced by rich countries, and it would be completely ineffective to enforce the kind of protectionism advocated by the remaining followers of Jean-Baptiste Colbert.

If terms such as "delocalization" and "unfair competition" ring true when applied to trading with poor countries, it is not because they correspond to the reality they are supposed to describe; it is because they fit the new internal reality of capitalism. The sudden "opening up" of capitalism is actually due to the impact of its own transformations. Globalization cannot be blamed for the emergence of smaller and more homogeneous production units, the increasing recourse to outsourcing, or the trend toward "task upgrading" (which leads to the rejection of less-skilled workers as so much deadwood). The changes currently underway affect every task in every sector and every trade, whether or not it is directly related to the global economy. Two major trends are responsible for these transformations: the information revolution and the advent of mass education. Each of these trends is, for the most part, independent of today's still-insignificant trade with poor countries.

It was long believed that Europe turned to its Atlantic shores as a result of the Turkish blockade of the Mediterranean in the sixteenth century, but Fernand Braudel's well-known research has now shown the opposite to be true: the Turks were able to seize control of the Mediterranean because European countries had lost interest in it.[2] Likewise, we now need to be lucid enough to reverse the commonly held argument that globalization is to be blamed for making today's labor market so insecure. On the contrary, it is our own propensity toward transforming the nature of work that has created a niche for "globalization" and given it an ominous dimension, causing some to reject it.

Pursuing the erroneous line of thought will place the battle for social welfare "on the sidelines" when it should be fought "on the inside." Such errors of analysis are not affordable; the stakes are too high.

1

The Poverty of the World

Now that communism is disappearing from the world stage, the West searches for new faces of evil. "What would Rome be without its enemies?" wondered Caton after the destruction of Carthage. "What will become of the West after the collapse of the East?" echoed Jean-Christophe Ruffin in a book eloquently titled *L'Empire et les Nouveaux Barbares*. His answer: "Prosperous and watchful, the Empire of the North works toward the same goal as each of its citizens: to last, and as long as possible, in the sweet warmth of wealth and peace."[1] The Roman Empire did fall—but, as Ruffin points out, not before five centuries had passed. The expectations of wealthy countries are not nearly as lofty today.

The belief that "globalization" will prevent them from enjoying the "sweet warmth of wealth and peace" is slowly forcing itself upon the wealthy nations. How can we trade with countries in which workers are not granted any social rights? Does trade with poor countries not expose rich countries to the risk of reverting to the "law of the market" as it imposed itself in the nineteenth century, at the dawn of European capitalism? We cannot answer these questions clearly until we understand why poor countries are poor and what specific role the world market plays in their rising prosperity.

The Poorest Person in the World

The displacement of peasants from their land, already a thing of the past in rich countries, is still at a very early stage in poor countries. Half of the world's population still lives in rural areas, and according to Henri Mendras the world has never had so many farmers.[2] In China and India 60 percent of the population is still rural; in Africa the figure is 70 percent. Chinese and Indian farmers earn approximately the equivalent of $1000–$2000 dollars per year, one-thirtieth what their European counterparts earn; on the other hand, they earn two to three times more than the world's very poorest peasants, most of whom live in Africa. The poorest person in the world, surely a woman, must be one of them. We can begin to delve into this African woman's daily life through the work of the agronomist René Dumont.[3]

Her daily walk to work takes more than 2 hours. She carries a load of up to 50 kilograms on her head, her youngest child on her back, and often another baby in her womb. In Zaire, 70 percent of domestic and production tasks are carried out by women. Young girls, beginning at age 10, are expected to help. They crush manioc and take care of the younger children. At age 14 they will be married (or, as Dumont writes, "raped rather than married"), or they may be sold into prostitution.

Dumont came across what he calls "leisure-class farmers" in a village in Senegal. Such a man keeps one of his wives with him, sending the others to work in the city for a year to earn money for the household. In the city, they sleep on the ground. They are fined by the police regularly. They work 12 hours a day, carrying their youngest children on their backs. Their nourishment is often limited to dry bread dipped in sugar water. When they return to the village a year later, their husband and their relatives judge them by the weight of the gifts they bring back.

Because of parasites, beasts of burden are seldom used in Africa. This is why the African economy has long been based on slavery. It would not be an exaggeration to say that African women are today's slaves.

Aside from being an insult to the rest of humanity, which hypocritically accepts its existence, the exploitation of women creates a self-perpetuating cycle of poverty: by making it unnecessary for a man to invest in machinery, it allows him to save enough money to buy another wife, who will bear more children, who will work for their father if they are boys and who will be sold if they are girls.

City and Countryside

The slavery of African women is only the first level of poverty in Africa. On the next level another form of exploitation is taking place: the entire countryside is exploited by the cities. According to a World Bank study, nearly half of the wealth produced by African farmers is appropriated by the cities.

This pattern of exploitation is carried out in a relatively transparent manner. At its center we commonly find state-owned bodies known as Marketing Boards, which are public agencies with a monopoly on the purchase of agricultural products.[4] Some of these boards were formed by farmers to stabilize the markets for raw materials. Others were established in the prewar years by large exporters as a way to exploit small farmers. During World War II these boards were often used by Great Britain to get supplies for British troops. In either case, upon gaining their independence after the war, African governments found themselves the inheritors of an efficient bureaucracy for agricultural production. They maintained this structure, arguing that the Marketing Boards could help the farmers to stabilize market prices for raw materials. The idea then was to stockpile commodities during healthy years and to return them to the producers during lean years.

But not everyone is able to act as Joseph did. The temptation to spend surpluses as soon as they accumulated became too strong. Farmers were forced to return all of their crops to the central authorities at the lowest possible prices. This soon enabled the Marketing Boards to start acting as strict supervisors of the production of farm commodities and raw materials.

A quasi-dictatorial body of laws gradually developed in order to keep the farmers from falling through the gaps of regulation. In Kenya, for example, the production of maize became subject to excessive regulation through the Maize Marketing Act, which stipulates that maize must be sold to the Marketing Board as soon as it has been harvested. All movements of maize require special permission from the government. The only exceptions are movement within the boundaries of a farm and movement by the owner exclusively for his own consumption—on the condition that it involve no more than two bags. Such regulations leave the farmers no alternative to the Marketing Board for the marketing of their products, thus allowing the government to dictate the lowest possible prices.

This hatred of the countryside has a simple origin: the elites are all urban, or at least derive all of their political legitimacy from the cities. Coups and revolutions originate in urban revolts. All the governments in the world dread the hunger riots that occur each time the International Monetary Fund tries to free the prices of food products. And so this urban sword of Damocles unleashes a vicious circle. By keeping the prices of agricultural products artificially low, the urban elites ruin the most vulnerable farmers, forcing them into cities, where they depend on subsidization of the prices of the farm goods they now must buy. If we consider that more than half of urban consumption consists of food products, we can fully appreciate both the irreversible nature and the absurdity of this process. Cities fill up with vagabonds and misfits, who become the underdogs of a policy of which they were the first victims. It becomes almost impossible to break this cycle: governments that attempt to do so are promptly repaid with urban riots. Poverty in the countryside—where, as already mentioned, the majority of the population resides—becomes irreversible.

Mercantilism

This confrontation between urban and rural areas has always been at the core of the human condition, from Jericho to Athens to Rome to the present day. Although today the world is characterized by the victory of cities over the countryside (the surest sign of decline, according to Spengler), it would be misinterpreting history and theory to think that current "urban" policies such as those carried out in Africa could speed up the birth of an industrial society. It may be in order to recall that the transition of European societies from an agrarian age to an industrial age was first thwarted by similar policies intended to favor the cities over the countryside.

For instance, in a disturbing parallel to African policies, the countries of Renaissance Europe had the same goal of maintaining the lowest possible prices for agricultural products. The movement of wheat was regulated in the same way; exportation was prohibited and importation was favored. Such policies were already practiced by the policy makers (Colbert and others) of sixteenth- and seventeenth-century Europe. This is what came to be known as mercantilism.

Mercantilism is a set of writings (rather than a doctrine as such) outlining what would today be called "economic policy." The term "political economy" (coined by the mercantilist thinker Antoine de Montchrestien) clearly defines the mercantilists' intent: to make the economy serve politics. How could it be done? The mercantilists' first objective was to maximize the inflow of gold into the country and to restrict its outflow. To this effect, they recommended prohibiting the exportation of gold. They also proposed fostering other exports through government support of a few monopolies which were charged with leading the "trade war." Finally, they suggested that imports be restricted so as to avoid wasting national wealth abroad.

Whether gains in wealth are pursued by subsidizing exports or by restricting imports, trade and industry are always the vector for gains in wealth according to mercantilist thought. Agriculture, however, suffers a different treatment: the exportation of wheat is prohibited, but its importation is favored. Although in Renaissance Europe (as in present-day Africa) 80 percent of the people were peasants, mercantilists upheld a theory of wealth in which agricultural production always came last. In *Essays on Mankind and Political Arithmetic* (written in 1671 and published in 1690), William Petty states that "there is much more to be gained by manufacture than husbandry; and by merchandise than manufacture." Agricultural production counts for little wealth in the mercantilist sense of the word. How was it possible for such a concept to occur to thinkers living in economies that were 80 percent rural?

In the case of Europe, it is easy to understand the foundations of mercantilist policies. First of all, policy makers were incredibly blind regarding the farming crisis. By the late fourteenth century, famines and epidemics had eliminated nearly 40 percent of Europe's population. Consequently, people became scarce and agriculture ceased to be a major concern. This was a gross miscalculation: as early as 1650, famines and epidemics returned to Europe.

And there is an even more fundamental explanation for the rise of mercantilism: by the late Middle Ages, Europe was defining its political boundaries. The mercantilists' recommendations were addressed to governments which were confronted with the pressing problem of finding fiscal resources that would allow them to wage progressively larger and costlier wars.[5] Competitive military buildups ruined the public finances of France, Spain and England. How would they cover these expenses? What fiscal resources could they use? The rural areas were the most populated, but the majority of the wealth produced there was also consumed there. How could a tax be levied on a farmer's products when the farmer was consuming nearly all of what he produced? Today such a policy would be tantamount to taxing household production in order to finance government spending. The monetary and fiscal wealth of rural areas was too meager. Cities, on the other hand, being the seats of industry and trade, were at the crossroads of an intricate network of market exchanges, and consequently they could depend on heavy taxation. Mercantilism thus suggested that kings rely on industry and trade to fill their coffers. Kings granted monopolies to guilds, to corporations of craftsmen, and to trade companies on the practice of their trades; in return they paid taxes, which quickly became the main source of revenue for governments. The rural contribution was to remain indirect: the prices of food products sold in the cities would be kept low, so that the urban population would be kept large and easy to feed.

However, cities cannot be helped by the pauperization of the countryside: sooner or later, famine will erupt as a consequence of a poorly controlled rural exodus. Urban populations can survive only to the extent that they can get food surpluses from the countryside—surpluses that can be abundant only if farmers are not being ruined. Such was the basic message that the physiocratic thinkers, led by François Quesnay, were to spread in the eighteenth century: abolishing the jumble of regulations that favored the cities, and assuming a "laissez-faire" attitude toward the natural equilibrium dictated by food production. This economic liberalism, which was to become the credo of nineteenth-century industrial societies, began to develop in the eighteenth century as a means of protecting rural areas.

And indeed historians are often of the opinion that advances in agriculture were among the major causes of the first industrial revolution, which occurred at the close of the eighteenth century. It was in rural areas that industrialization first developed (by means of what would later be called "proto-industrialization"). This was due to the leisure time that became available to farmers once their agricultural production increased (as a result of a better-controlled balance between the production of industrial goods—most often textiles—and the production of foodstuffs). This framework still operates today: it is the implicit point of reference for development in Asia. The same World Bank study that concluded that African agriculture was being plundered also revealed that in Korea the rural areas were subsidized by the cities. Evidently, Asian farmers do not allow the cities to dictate their prices. Deng's China also conformed to this physiocratic model of development, having allowed agricultural prosperity to develop as a basis for industrialization.

The African countries might be said to have remained outside this model of development. Starved for fiscal resources, like the mercantilist states, but also drunk with corruption, African countries are impoverishing their rural areas, in the noble tradition inaugurated by the kings of the Old Regime.

Corruption

At the third level of African life, economic elites are exploiting entire nations. "What serious man does not invest a portion of his wealth in Switzerland?" is a remark attributed to Houphouet Boigny,[6] who, backing up his words with actions, established daily flights between Abidjan and Geneva. The swindling of Africans by their leaders is known only too well. Mobutu Sese Seko of Zaire was no doubt one of the wealthiest individuals in the world, along with the heads of state of other developing countries. These despots are not content with surreptitiously exacting a percentage of the wealth produced. They are driving the countries they govern into the most extreme poverty, wasting any existing mining or oil resources.

Victor Naim's analysis of the Venezuelan experience contains the following summary statement, which can be applied to many developing countries: "In a striking example of a reversed-Midas touch, the system had systematically turned gold—or oil—into poverty."[7] The way in which Venezuela depleted its enormous oil revenue is a perfect example of the effects of corruption in a number of developing countries. In the second half of the 1970s, rising oil prices enabled the Venezuelan government to set up investment funds which were supposed to support the industrialization of the country. In parallel with the case of the Marketing Boards in Africa, these public funds were quickly diverted by the lobbies surrounding Carlos Andrès Perès, who was Venezuela's president at the time. Overambitious projects were undertaken in a mad race for kickbacks and commissions, with practically no regard for economic efficiency. The construction of aluminum and steel plants which the country definitely did not need was only a cover for the diverting of public funds. As a result, Venezuela became poor over the period 1970–1990 in spite of its oil resources. It became poorer not only in relation to other countries, but in the absolute: the average income of a Venezuelan was lower in 1990 than it was in 1970. Corruption had damaged the economy in such a way as to make it less productive than it had been 20 years earlier.

The same situation prevails in Nigeria, for the same reasons. Oil revenues led the government to build a new capital city from scratch, and this promptly led to an enormous waste of wealth. According to an estimate published by Nigeria's Ministry of Finance, only 500 million of the 23 billion nairas invested can be considered to have been invested wisely.

Other examples of this "reverse Midas touch" abound.[8] At the core of the process, we always find the same chain of events: a corrupt power initiates wasteful expenditures in order to divert public funds, investment funds are immediately squandered, and social programs are diverted from their original purposes.

"Democracy for Africa"

As David Landes has noted, a feature of the modern Western world is that "the ruler abandoned, voluntarily or involuntarily, the right or practice of arbitrary or indefinite disposition of the wealth of his subjects." It first happened when the British Parliament put limitations on the king's power to make fiscal decisions; then came the American Revolution in reaction to King George's taxation; then the French Revolution which abolished the fiscal privileges of aristocrats. The history of today's democracies reflects this long battle against the ruler's discretionary power over taxation.

One could say that African societies have reached a crossroads resembling the aforementioned points in history.[9] When René Dumont pleads in favor of "democracy for Africa," he does so on the basis of a set of rigorous arguments against the exploitation of women, the exploitation of rural areas, and the corruption of the elites. Through democracy, education becomes a credible objective. Thanks to education, especially of women, a society could move on to other kinds of material and educational wealth accumulation. Educational attainment and a democratic system would eventually reinforce one another, allowing for abolition or containment of the elites' discretionary power.

It is disturbing to note the extent to which some of the statements recently made by René Dumont, an agronomist by training, coincide with those of Quesnay, the eighteenth-century physiocrat. Both thinkers denounce urban mercantilism as the oppressor of the countryside. Quesnay was not a democrat, but he believed that the free play of markets would be sufficient to "emancipate" humanity. He is the author of entries on "grains" and "farmers" in Diderot's Encyclopedia. His representation may be considered rather naive today, given the hindsight that nineteenth-century history provides regarding the destitution that can be wrought by a market left to its own will. But this type of discourse is anything but obsolete: today, far from Africa, it finds a resounding echo in Asia.

2

A Tale of Two Cities

According to Paul Bairoch, "there were no great differences in levels of income between various civilizations at the moment they reached their peak: first-century Rome, tenth-century Arabic Caliphates, eleventh-century China, seventeenth-century India, and eighteenth-century Europe."[1] At the dawn of the first industrial revolution, the gap in per-capita income between Western Europe and India, Africa, or China was probably no more than 30 percent. All this changed abruptly with the industrial revolution. In 1870 the per capita income of the wealthiest countries was already 11 times that of the poorest. By 1995, the wealthiest were more than 50 times as rich as the poorest. The phenomenon of disparity between countries is therefore "recent," having developed over the last two centuries.

By the early 1980s the idea that we might witness a convergence of the revenues of rich and poor countries had become unthinkable, since the widening of the gap between the richest and the poorest was apparently the rule of economic development. Toward the middle of the 1980s, however, economists noticed a trend in statistical data which they dubbed "conditional convergence": through investment, education, and trade, poor countries could manage to catch up with rich countries. This is exactly the formula that was used in Asia—initially in

Japan, then in four countries regarded by many Westerners as the Horsemen of the Apocalypse: Hong Kong, Singapore, South Korea, and Taiwan—in a process that is now being closely examined by the rest of the world. Could the accomplishments of these four countries (whose combined populations do not exceed 80 million) be repeated at the level of the entire Asian continent, and even beyond? The probable answer is Yes, as evidenced by the two most extreme cases of such gains in wealth: Hong Kong and Singapore.[2]

Hong Kong and Singapore

Immediately after World War II, these two big shantytowns were used by the British as warehouses for their trade with China (in the case of Hong Kong) and with Malaysia or Indonesia (in the case of Singapore). By now, each has become wealthier than its former master, and each has a higher per-capita income. Singapore is one of the ten wealthiest countries in the world, on a par with Canada; Hong Kong comes close, being on the same level as Italy.

In the early postwar years, Hong Kong fared better than Singapore. Shortly after the Chinese Revolution of 1949, hundreds of thousands of refugees flowed into the city—among them a large number of former entrepreneurs from Shanghai. These immigrants, having brought with them a great deal of industrial know-how, promptly reconstructed an industrial base that put Hong Kong on the path to what later became the *cursus honorum* of the developing countries. At first, the industrialization of Hong Kong was based on textiles. Then, as industrialized countries reinforced their protectionism, the city moved into more elaborate production, expanding into the clothing industry, in which it is more difficult for protectionism to set efficient norms. Throughout the 1970s Hong Kong gradually extended its range of activities, soon becoming the world's leading manufacturer of toys and one of the leading exporters of electronic products (quartz watches in particular).

In the early 1980s, at the peak of Hong Kong's industrialization, China embarked on a course of economic liberalization. In a twist of fate, people returned to Shanghai from Hong Kong to recreate capitalism as they knew it in pre-Mao China, and Hong Kong began to revert to its former role as a warehouse for trade between China and the rest of the world.

Singapore's postwar experience was far more difficult. The educational attainment of the population was one of the lowest in the world,[3] and the political climate was very unstable. The city was shaken by a communist insurrection in Malaysia in the 1950s, then by a war between Indonesia and Malaysia in the 1960s. In 1967, when Great Britain decided to withdraw its military personnel from the city, industrialization had not yet taken off. The year 1967 was a turning point for Singapore: the iron-fisted Lee Kuan Yew took charge of the city.

The Singaporean government promulgated a series of quasi-dictatorial reforms. Labor legislation was "simplified" in such a way that all labor disputes were submitted to the judgment of an industrial court of arbitration whose mission was to watch over the "interests of the community as a whole." The government also launched a radical reform regarding public funds. In the early 1970s, the government was able to avail itself of a surplus of public funds in excess of 10 percent of the gross domestic product. The mandatory pension funds plan that was later established financed, by itself, half of the investment in the city throughout the 1970s and the 1980s. Finally, the government offered foreign investors tax exemptions of up to 90 percent on profits generated. As a result, Singapore became the leading recipient of international investments in the world. According to a recent United Nations study, Singapore has actually received, in the 1980s and the first half of the 1990s, close to $60 billion in external investments—nearly 50 percent more than Indonesia (which has 30 times Singapore's population) and 20 times as much as India.

Singapore's government increased industrial subsidies, taking advantage of its considerable internal and external resources. After first focusing on textiles, it turned to chemicals and oil, then to toys, then to electronics and computers, and finally (in the early 1990s) to financial services.

Between 1970 and 1980, Singapore's output of televisions increased by a factor of 50. In the early 1980s, Singapore had absolutely no computer experience; by the late 1980s it had become the leading exporter of hard disks in the world. Equally impressive is Singapore's development from a place with very little financial activity into one of the most active financial centers in Asia.[4]

The rate at which Singapore's government pushes its industries forward is spectacular and, according to many observers, almost absurd. None of the industries has enough time to consolidate its advantages before the government, in a mad race, is already moving on to the next stage of specialization. And yet, this can be said to have worked. The fast pace of decisions regarding specialization, while unrealistic at every stage, has enabled Singapore to become one of the wealthiest cities in the world.

Can We Generalize?

A number of countries, in Asia and elsewhere, are already using Hong Kong and Singapore as points of reference. Consider, for example, the African island of Mauritius.[5]

Much like Singapore in its "early days," Mauritius went through a period of political instability after achieving independence in 1968. The situation was so precarious that the future Nobel Prize winner James Meade, who wrote a report on the island's prospects for development, concluded that considerable pay cuts could not be avoided. The political crisis culminated when a state of emergency was declared and a number of party and union leaders were sent to prison. From 1978 to 1982, the island was affected by the falling prices of sugar, its primary export. In 1982, when a democratically elected government came to power, the rate of declared unemployment was 20 percent. From then on, the situation on Mauritius changed radically. The government decided to play the card of developing unrestricted (tariff-free) zones. With the support of industrialists from Hong Kong who saw Mauritius as offering a way to get around the restrictions imposed on their own exports, the government succeeded in multiplying the island's textile production by 5. At the end of a decade of accelerated growth, Mauritius succeeded in doubling the purchasing power of its wage earners, thus widening the gap between itself and its African neighbors. Anyone attempting to predict the growth pattern of Mauritius on the basis of its low levels of education and equipment or on the basis of its political history would have concluded, as did James Meade, that it was headed for disaster.

These examples all show that the "poverty traps" whose logic we saw at work in the case of Africa can be avoided.

Even Singapore's extremely unfavorable initial conditions— no previous industrialization and no educated population—did not prevent the city from taking off economically. However, in light of the methods used by the Singaporean government, one should avoid any naively enthusiastic judgments based on this particular model of development. At stake in this discussion is the *feasibility* of the process rather than its desirability. It is one thing to advocate or criticize the methods used in Singapore; it is another to infer from the analysis of "objective conditions" that economic growth is impossible, whether it is wanted or not. It is one thing to criticize Lee Kuan Yew's methods; it is another to understand why such methods bring wealth to Asia but poverty to Africa.

The Wealth of Nations

Economists usually distinguish three factors of production in determining the wealth of a nation: labor, capital, and technological progress. Capital and labor are evaluated by conventional means. Capital is measured by adding up the country's investments, adjusted for depreciation and obsolescence. Labor is represented by the number of person-hours as corrected, through dubious but generally similar methods, by an indicator of workers' educational attainment. Technological progress, which is also designated as "total factor productivity," measures the efficiency with which an economy combines capital and labor. If, for example, two economies invest the same amounts of capital and recruit the same number of workers, but one is still poorer than the other, the poorer economy is said to have a lower level of "total factor productivity." By the same token, if the growth of one economy decreases over time despite the fact that it is maintaining the previous rates of investment and recruitment, it is said that the rate of growth of its total factor productivity has diminished. Thus, "total productivity" is a sort of black box to which economists relegate anything that cannot be accounted for either by labor or by capital accumulation.

Whenever the sources of growth have been decomposed into labor, capital, and total factor productivity, economists have been astounded to discover that productivity ("technological progress") consistently plays a role at least as important as those of the traditional factors of production. For example, during the period 1950–1973, when France "caught up with" the United States, increases in productivity accounted for 60 percent of France's economic growth. In most other industrialized countries, too, technological progress represents close to half of postwar economic growth.

How does this decomposition play out in the case of the Four Tigers? Does most of their gain in wealth automatically result from the increased use of manpower and machinery, or should it be attributed to their "total productivity"? Let us closely examine the forces in play.

If the wealth of the Four Tigers were due mainly to their specialization strategies, to the niches they have established in the world market, or even to the advantages resulting from their "Asian values," we would have to conclude that their productivity growth has been very strong. But in fact we discover that exactly the reverse is true. When the countries of the world are ranked in terms of their total growth, the Four Tigers (Hong Kong, Singapore, South Korea, and Taiwan) are among the five most productive countries in the world (Botswana being number 1 because of its diamond mines). But when we rank them in terms of the technological progress from which they have benefited, the order is upset: instead of being good students, the Four Tigers now appear mediocre, with the dunce cap going to Singapore (which, over the last 20 years, has registered no technological progress).

As can be seen from the accompanying table, the Four Tigers' growth is almost entirely attributable to their *domestic* efforts. In his discussion of these data, Paul Krugman states that the Tigers owe their wealth to perspiration rather than to

Table 2.1
Growth rates, in percent. Sources: for Asia, Alwyn Young: "A tale of two cities," in *NBER Macroeconomic Annual 1992*; for France, Angus Maddison, *Dynamic Forces in Capitalist Development* (Oxford University Press, 1991), p. 158, table 5.19.

	Total growth	Capital input	Labor input	Total productivity growth
South Korea	10.3	4.6	4.5	1.2
Taiwan	9.4	3.2	3.6	2.6
Singapore	8.7	5.6	2.9	0.2
Hong Kong	7.3	3.0	2.0	2.3
France (1950–1973)	5.0	1.8	0.2	3.0

inspiration.[6] The example of Singapore is the most striking: nearly two-thirds of its growth results from its extraordinary saving rate. In both South Korea and Taiwan, nearly three-fourths of the growth originates from capital and labor. Hong Kong stands out, for the reasons noted above (the large human capital from the start), as having experienced more balanced growth, with each of the three factors accounting for one-third. In a nutshell, development in Asia has basically been achieved through saving. China is perfectly representative of this strategy: in 1995 the rate of saving was 43 percent of national revenues, versus 16 percent in Sub-Saharan Africa in the same year.

As this comparison makes clear, the "miracle" of the Four Tigers is simple to understand: there is no miracle. As is pointed out in the writings of Adam Smith and Martin Luther, wealth repays each individual's efforts. This is the great message of hope for countries that want to follow these principles. The simplest solutions—encouraging saving and investment and educating the workforce—clearly seem to allow poor countries to catch up with rich countries.

Wealth and International Trade

In light of the preceding, what should we think of the Four Tigers' choice to gear their development toward world trade? Obviously the contribution of export strategies to their industrial success should not be ignored. A counterexample is provided by the countries of the former Soviet Union, whose decisions went the opposite way; they indicate that catching up with the richest countries takes more than educating the workforce and pushing for rapid industrialization of the economy. The "industrializing industrialization" that the French economist Gaston de Bernis recommended for Algeria in 1971, and the undeniable efforts made there in the area of mass education, did not result in Algeria's catching up to the industrialized countries; they resulted in excess production capacity and in joblessness among educated workers (and thus in recruits for the Islamic Salvation Front). What are we to make of the difference between these "introverted" industrializing strategies and those chosen by the Tigers?

The answer probably is as follows: Thanks to the world market, it took Asian countries only a few years to gain access to a market economy that Western countries had spent more than a century setting up. Recall the innumerable anecdotes regarding the Soviet Union: if the planners base the production goals for statues of Lenin on volume, the statues will be in abundant supply but crumbly; if the goals are based on weight, there will be few statues but each will be preposterously heavy. A "market" is what prevents the relationship between producers and consumers from being subject to manipulation: it is a coherent system of prices and standards of quality. Thus, Asian countries are clearly importing a market "structure" rather than market "shares."

In this respect, it is interesting to note how insignificant the domestic choices made by Taiwan, South Korea, Hong Kong, and Singapore have been, since each of these countries has accepted the world market's requirements regarding prices and quality. In Hong Kong, the only role played by government was to administer the leasing of land (which nominally remained its exclusive property). In South Korea, on the other hand, development centered around several large combines, whose lobbying power was crudely brought to light by the indictment of two former presidents for corruption. Furthermore, unlike Taiwan's government, South Korea's government was "protectionist" for a long time, protecting national enterprises from foreign competition at its discretion. We should not let ourselves be deluded by the economic "liberalism" of Asian countries. The government is often the principal player in growth strategies. If we can still speak of liberalism, it is because of the fundamental role played by the world market in the validation of the chosen strategies. In spite of its planned character, the Korean strategy yields to market prices and regulations in order to trade Korean goods. Therefore, protectionism does not have the same consequences in Korea as in Zaire. The same holds true for corruption: in South Korea it is only one part of an overall process subject to exterior rules; in Zaire it has no limits.

The world market's key role in the internal organization of Asian economies is perfectly illustrated by the example of China. As the most populous nation in the world, it would follow according to traditional economic logic, China should also be one of the most closed economies in the world, since a country is usually less inclined to trade with the rest of the world when it has a vast economy of its own. For instance, the United States and Brazil engage in limited external trading, whereas France trades a lot and Belgium even more. But China, which was still one of the most closed countries in the world in 1975 (with an import rate under 5 percent), now does as much trading, in proportion to its wealth, as France (with an import rate of approximately 20 percent). One reason for this opening to trade is the simple fact that Chinese inter-province trade often operates through the world market. According to Alwyn Young, rather than think of China as a country of 1.2 billion inhabitants, it may be better to represent it as 25 separate provinces, each composed of 50 million inhabitants and trading with the rest of the world.[7]

The Golden Age to Come

According to the World Bank, the rate of growth in Asia could reach an average of 7.5 percent per year over the next 20 years. Annual growth rates of 10 percent—previously unobserved, even during Europe's postwar "golden age"—have already become the norm in China, Thailand, and Malaysia. An exceptional push forward, inconceivable just 15 years earlier, is underway. Evidently a "catching up" phenomenon is at work, replicating on a much grander scale the mechanism that permitted postwar Europe and Japan to catch up to the United States. This slowly emerging movement toward a narrowing of the gap between rich and poor countries is what might be called the great hope of the twenty-first century. If it were to happen, it would perhaps one day allow historians to conclude that the nineteenth and twentieth centuries were but a parenthesis in the history of countries. The nearly exclusive privilege bestowed upon the West by the industrial revolution would then have lasted just long enough to give the other civilizations a chance to adjust to it.

Will economic catching up also be accompanied by political catching up? I touched on the question of democracy in the context of Africa. But the diagnosis must be modified for Asia, where democracy has not been a trigger for growth as it was in the West, or as it might be in Africa, but where democracy may result from growth that is already underway.

In purely economic terms, democracy in Asia has been long in coming because conflicts over redistribution have not been as acute as in Africa or in Latin America. First, as was stated in chapter 1, the conflict between city and countryside is not as harsh in Asia as in Africa. Second, differences in income are less pronounced: South Korea and Taiwan are among the most egalitarian countries in the world—more egalitarian than France, and almost on a par with Sweden. Finally, the issue of educational attainment, which is obviously of critical importance to social justice, has most often been given appropriate consideration in Asia: education imposed itself quickly, in the name of the growth imperative. Education, having emerged as a crucial factor in economic development, can also be seen as a possible future trigger for reconsideration of political issues. In a capitalist world in which education necessarily takes on a general, universal form (rather than the specific form of trades transmitted from one generation to the next, as in a pre-industrial economy), it is truly difficult to resist the conclusion that higher educational attainment will sooner or later lead to strong democratic aspirations.

Should capitalism and democracy be exported to developing countries, would the cultures of these countries automatically have to adopt the Western model and give up their own values, or might we witness a subtler dialectic allowing each culture to be preserved while absorbing the rules of the global market? Japan has long been cited as the first Asian country to have understood all the benefits it could derive from entering the world market while managing to preserve its culture. Today, however, the verdict on the preservation of traditional Japanese values is no longer as clear. The foundations of Japanese culture (respect for authority and the second-class status of women) are crumbling, with higher educational standards for women playing a fundamental role in the process. To put it in now-conventional terms, as expressed by Louis Dumont, we can say that the hierarchic society of Japan is gradually vanishing, to be replaced by a more egalitarian society in which the market economy plays a powerful role.[8]

In fact, the central paradox of the debate over globalization has to do with the difficult position in which Western countries seem to find themselves as they try to absorb the shock of emerging globalization. Today it is in rich countries—no longer in poor countries—that globalization causes fear. Like a boomerang thrown too accurately, the Western model comes back to its creators. Should rich countries prepare to accept the law of a market economy which they created, just as ancient Greek cities submitted to the yoke of a Roman empire which had adopted their gods?

3

The Great Fear of the Western World

"During the past few years, 4 billion people have suddenly entered the world economy," states Sir James Goldsmith, who goes on to say that "these new entrants into the world economy are in direct competition with the workforces of developed countries. They have become part of the same global labor market."[1] So we are warned. Equally threatening words were spoken in 1992 by the independent candidate Ross Perot, who ran against Bill Clinton and George Bush for the US presidency, when the North American Free Trade Agreement was about to be signed. Perot stated that he could hear the "giant sucking sound" of US markets being gobbled up by Mexican production. He predicted that US products would suddenly lose all their competitiveness when faced with their Southern competitors, and that the US economy would be left with the sad choice of either closing up shop or falling in line with Mexico. But exactly the opposite has occurred: Mexico has experienced enormous deficits and, as a result, has undergone a huge financial crisis and a spectacular collapse of the peso.

And yet everyone knew (or should have known) that before the crisis the peso was overvalued. Despite alarmism about Mexican workers' low wages, a "strong" peso enabled Americans to invade the Mexican market. It took the financial crisis for the peso to become "weak," which allowed Mexico to release surpluses in order to repay its debts. The lesson of this story is universal: there is always a rate of exchange in relation to which sales and purchases of goods balance out, and the fear of a loss of "global" competitiveness is therefore absurd. More precisely, as is evidenced by the example of Mexico, it is possible for exchange-rate disequilibria to occur, but they are usually promptly corrected. As David Hume stated as early as 1742 in his essays on commerce, the immediate consequence of flourishing trade in a nation is that the abundance of gold raises the price of the nation's commodities, "enabling the poorer states to undersell the richer in all foreign markets."[2] This says it all, as long as the monetary adjustments discussed by Hume are understood as fluctuations of exchange rather than as fluctuations of gold.

It is therefore not a "global" deficit in their trade with poor countries that rich countries should fear. If a poor country sells $100 worth of goods to a rich country, sooner or later it will also buy $100 worth of goods. Indeed, it did not take long for historians who looked closely at the worrisome estimates made by Pliny the Elder[3] to discover that he took into account only the Romans' purchases, to the exclusion of their sales. Had Pliny estimated what Asia or Arabia spent on Roman products, he would have given a more sober report: on average, the Romans' sales compensated their purchases.[4] At stake here is not the disequilibrium between sales and purchases, but the *sectorial composition* of the two: which sectors will be sellers and which will be buyers.

Comparative Advantage

Hume's essay has remained well known in the history of thought because it is one of the sharpest critiques of the mercantilist position, which upholds the opposite view: that it is possible and mostly desirable to have infinite surpluses. The mercantilists' obsession with deficits is attributable primarily to their era's preoccupation with gold and silver. As William Petty notes, "the great and ultimate effect of trade is not wealth at large, but particularly abundance of silver, gold and jewels, which are not perishable, nor so mutable as other commodities, but are wealth at all times, and in all places: whereas abundance of wine, corns, fowls, flesh, etc. are riches but *hic et nunc.*"[5] Following Petty's train of thought, we could almost liken wealth to a treasure hunt in which the winner is the first sailor to find the treasure. Competition is always bad when one is engaged in a search for buried treasure. It may be good to charter other boats for one's own use, but it is always bad when others do the same: they threaten to be the first to find the treasure. Herein lies the simple explanation for the mercantilists' belief that international competition is always bad.

These remarks make it easier to understand why the classical thinkers Smith and Ricardo, who were to reinvent political economy in the eighteenth and nineteenth centuries as a reaction to mercantilism, first applied themselves to revising the definition of wealth. For Smith and Ricardo (and for Malthus), the wealth of a nation is to be gauged not by its stockpiles of gold, but by the labor of its people and by the means it has to make optimum use of its labor force. This approach obviously modifies our perspective on the mercantilists' "treasure hunt" radically. I should no longer worry that foreign competition will steal my treasure, since my treasure is my work, which no one can take away from me, and which I am always totally free to apply to tasks that make the best possible use of it. This is an issue of great importance; addressing it was to be the main contribution of the classical economists (Ricardo in particular) who devised what later came to be known as the theory of *comparative advantage.*

Adam Smith characterized the modern world as one in which each individual specializes in one task and leaves the rest to the markets. The logic leading to such specialization is simple: I choose the trade at which, in comparison with other trades, I am most competent. I may very well be an excellent pastry chef and an excellent shoemaker at the same time—perhaps an even better pastry chef than the one who sells me pastry. No matter: If I perform better as a shoemaker than as a pastry chef, I will spend all my time making shoes, and I will buy my pastry. The income I draw from the activity at which I excel will necessarily pay for the time which I would have spent in making my own bread. I can, of course, be nostalgic about the time when I made my own bread. This nostalgia, however, will never be strong enough to actually make me do it. This longing for the past can be very intense precisely because none of us really wants the past to come back. As Ricardo stated, trade between countries will obey similar principles: each nation will specialize in the area in which it can use *comparative* advantage. Thus, although a certain country may excel in both agricultural productivity and industrial productivity, if industrial production is what it is best at relative to other countries it will profit by importing food so that it can specialize in industry.

History has shown itself to be cruel in this respect. The idea that trade is a factor of self-fulfillment in all places and at all times is theoretically naive and historically false. As Great Britain specializes in industrial production, it imports agricultural products, ruining its farming population. Inversely, when Southern countries trade with Great Britain, they import British products, disrupting their cottage industries. In both cases the transition is cruel for those who take a direct hit from the reconversion resulting from trade. It may be appropriate at this point to recall how "globalization" came about in the nineteenth century, in the wake of the first industrial revolution. It will help us understand why the countries of the South have long feared trading with the North, and why so many people argue that it is now the Northern countries' turn to be fearful of such trading.

Trade as a Destructive Force

In the early nineteenth century, Ricardo demonstrated how Great Britain should leave agriculture to other countries and specialize in the area in which it was comparatively the best, namely industry. This was no sooner said than done. At the beginning of the eighteenth century the British population was 70 percent rural, but by 1840 that percentage was down to 25. By the end of the nineteenth century, Britain's rural population had all but vanished.

A reading of the works of Dickens or Marx reveals the harshness of this transition. For the generation on the front lines, the consequences of Ricardo's theory were devastating. The replacement of domestic products with imported foodstuffs could not be stopped. The farmers who had been ruined by this competition were forced to leave the countryside and seek factory work in cities, where they experienced unhealthy conditions and destitution, discovering the precariousness of working-class life. According to Jean Fourastié, "the drama of transitional situations can be illustrated by a move from an isolated farm in Quercy [a region of France], where the way of life has not changed since Virgil, to the dysfunctional suburbs of a large Northern city."[6] In order to fully grasp the nature of this drama, let us examine the Southern part of Ricardo's program.[7]

When Great Britain decided to abandon agriculture and specialize in industrial production, it had to find countries that were headed in the opposite direction and willing to "deindustrialize." What countries were candidates? Not the other European countries, which were counting on catching up with British industrialization and were therefore closing their borders to British products. In practice, trade could occur only with countries that were under British rule. When India was flooded with British products, the result was a total destruction of its industrial base. Early in the nineteenth century, India was a net exporter of textiles. "Printed calico," a silk fabric, was in great demand, and India's cottage industry was well developed. By the end of the century, three-fourths of the textiles consumed by India were imported from Great Britain. True to Ricardo's theory, India was deindustrializing as a counterpart to British industrialization.

But the tragedy did not stop there. Which products would give India the best comparative advantage? Not wheat or other food crops; Great Britain preferred to buy these from the United States, at least until the Civil War. India was better at exporting cotton, jute, and indigo. A new outcome of trade was that India, the granary of Asia early in the nineteenth century, became specialized in the cultivation of products that no longer guaranteed its own food supply, and consequently was made to import basic products. It did not take long for famines to come as a result of this specialization: each time the world's state of affairs was unfavorable, India found itself unable to afford to import food.

Unfortunately, the drama of the theory of comparative advantage extends even further. The British discovered that the Indians excelled at cultivating the poppy plant, for which the main market was nearby China. To the detriment of free trade, the Chinese were aware of the devastating effects of opium on their population and wanted to forbid its trade. No matter: Great Britain declared war on China in order to force it to open its ports to poppy imports. The Treaty of Nankin, signed in 1842, concluded the "Opium Wars" to the advantage of Great Britain and free trade: opium was free to enter China. It has taken a century and a Communist revolution to counter the disastrous effects of this.

The dubious chronicles of the theory of comparative advantage are peppered with a thousand other examples. From Ceylon (which was forced to abandon all crops except for tea) to the Ottoman Empire and Latin America (both of which lost their industrial bases over the course of the nineteenth century), most of today's Third World countries have felt the deindustrializing impact of trading with Great Britain, the leading industrial country of the nineteenth century.

Such events account for what, for the sake of simplicity, I will call *the fear of deindustrialization*—a fear that can be attributed to Ricardo's suggestion that one country's industrialization implies the deindustrialization of another country. This fear is a reflection of the idea that the international division of labor limits some countries to secondary activities that do not provide any impetus for the rest of their economies and that reserves "industrializing industrialism"[8] for the richest countries.

The New Deindustrialization

The extremely traumatic nature of "globalization" for Third World countries in the nineteenth century led them to think that they would benefit by choosing to pursue "self-centered" strategies—that is, development strategies operating beyond the reach of world trade. Today, poor countries, looking at the

Four Tigers of Asia, understand that they can rely on world trade to support their industrialization. A fundamental qualitative change has already come about: between 1970 and 1990, the portion of exports from developing countries represented by manufactured products grew from 20 percent to 60 percent. The image of a developing country specializing in exporting primary products has disappeared. In 1990, 17 percent of the labor force in Third World countries and in former planned economies was already working, directly or indirectly, in an industrial export sector. Everything indicates that poor countries want to reinforce this trend.

The fear of trade persists, but it has suddenly changed camps. From now on, rich countries will be the ones fearing that "globalization" is a harbinger of their deindustrialization. They are the ones that tried to reinstate protectionism in the 1980s. What are we to think of this emerging fear? Let us keep in mind the theory of comparative advantage, which has until now served as our guide. It is obvious that world trade has become one of the engines of the industrialization of the South, and that one of its consequences is a partial deindustrialization of the North. However, it is also obvious that this process will not bring the countries of the North back to the countryside. The industrialization of the South is nudging the North toward a specialization of exchanges in which the North exports sophisticated goods. The fear of "old-style," regressive, "deindustrializing" deindustrialization is therefore not the point at stake in rich countries. Whole sectors of traditional industry in rich countries are threatened by the process now underway. As in the case of British farmers in the nineteenth century, some workers are going to have to leave what had gradually become, since that era, the reassuring framework of working-class life. Century-old industries, such as textiles, clothing, steel mills, and shipyards, are forced to close under the pressure of the South. But inversely, new skills, new industries, high-speed trains, software, etc. are making great strides owing to the outlets offered to them by developing countries. If we keep away from the fear of deficits, we know that these new outlets (whatever they may be) will be roughly equivalent *in value* to imported products. But if we have learned the lesson of the nineteenth century, we also know that world trade can have *redistributive* effects of great magnitude in every country. What will be the "net" effect of contemporary global exchanges? Who will win and who will lose as a result of these transformations?

Macroeconomic Adjustment

In the standard theory of international trade as it was developed by neo-Ricardian thinkers, the consequences of trading with poor countries are analyzed as follows[9]: In an industrial world no longer concerned with agriculture, neo-Ricardian economists consider rich countries as having a comparative advantage in the production of goods with "high added value"— that is, goods that require little labor but a great deal of capital (much machinery)—and poor countries as having a comparative advantage in the production of goods that utilize a great deal of labor and little capital. Trade between rich and poor countries therefore will induce disequilibrium in the job market of rich countries. Few jobs are in fact created by exports, and many are eliminated as a result of imports from the South. Hence, two factors will combine and operate against labor "in general" and in favor of capital. Workers who lose their jobs as a result of imports from the South will have to find new jobs; by so doing, they will push wages down, and capitalists will take advantage of these circumstances to improve their profit margins. These profit margins will continue to grow for the following reason: since export sectors use a great deal of capital, contrary to the working population, capitalists will profit from higher demand; capital will be scarce and therefore costly, and capitalists will again be the great beneficiaries of globalization. This analysis sometimes leads to statements that globalization operates in favor of capital and against workers, and that it is the manner in which capitalists impose "wage restraint" on workers and thus improve their profits.

However, the "proof" according to which globalization operates "at the expense of" workers in rich countries is completely false. It is grounded in the idea that Northern countries export capital-intensive goods and import labor-intensive goods. But this is quite simply not the case. As early as 1955, Wassily Leontief made a rigorous comparison of the labor share and the capital share in the United States' trade with other countries, and found the proportions to be exactly the reverse of those predicted by the theory. The United States, the richest country in the world, exports goods that are more labor intensive than those it buys from outside its borders. "Leontief's paradox" (as his model is known) was devastating[10]: the commodities exported by the rich countries require much labor and little capital.

If capital does not fully account for the North-South difference, what does? What comparative advantage of the North (relative to the South) is responsible for the structure of exchanges? The answer is close at hand: the North's comparative advantage lies in the greater proportion of skilled labor in its working population.

Economists have reexamined the data on export and import in light of this new decomposition, examining the share of skilled labor in a country's exports and the share of unskilled labor in its imports. For a vast majority of rich countries, the outcome is quite convincing: exports consume more skilled labor than average production does, and conversely imports consume a much higher share of unskilled labor. As predicted by the "naive" theory of international commerce, whenever a rich country trades with a poor country, buying and selling $100 worth of goods, the number of jobs created by exporting is smaller than the number of jobs eliminated by importing. But the reason is not that the $100 in exports remunerates labor poorly and capital well; it is that exports will provide better pay for a smaller number of hours worked by a more highly skilled person. If exports are profitable for skilled workers and detrimental to unskilled workers, we should not fear that trade will create a distortion in the ratio of wages to profits; rather, we should fear that it will result in greater disparities in wages. It is within the world of work that we must look for the consequences of globalization.

New Comparative Advantages

A very convincing way of approaching the effect of the world market on the labor markets of rich countries is to adopt the typology proposed by Robert Reich in *The Work of Nations*.[11] Reich divides American society into four categories.

Reich's first category consists of "symbolic analysts"—the "problem brokers" whose activities are directly tied to the global economy. Members of this group enjoy all the benefits of "globalization." One might say that this group comprises all who are offered new opportunities of exchange and production by globalization—users of the Internet, for instance.

The second category consists of educators, health-care workers, and all others who contribute directly or indirectly to the welfare state or have activities related to it. In Marxist language, they could be said to fulfill production and reproduction functions for the working class: education, health care, retirement, and so on. (In France, most of these individuals would work for the government; in the United States, many of them are in the private sector.)

Reich's third category consists of "in-person" service workers, such as restaurant workers and housecleaners.

The fourth category is made up of what Reich calls "routine producers": the "key punchers" of the service industry who enter data into computers and all others who are at risk of "delocalization" because their work is repetitive and does not require any special skills or any person-to-person relationships with clients.

The symbolic analysts are guaranteed to benefit from globalization; the routine producers are guaranteed to suffer from it. Will members of the other two groups be helped by the prosperity of the first group, or will they be subject to deflationary competition from members of the last group (who are now redundant)? The answer to this question will depend on the intensity of the mechanisms that are at work and on the demographic evolution of the various groups.

"Symbolic Analysts"

By what mechanisms does "globalization" lead to a gain in wealth for the symbolic analysts (as Reich calls them)? Within the framework of Ricardian theory, it would at first appear that these individuals now constitute the comparative advantage of rich countries: their products benefit from increasing demand by poor countries, a phenomenon that automatically raises their welfare. The exact relationship between producers of "symbols" (that is, ideas) and globalization is subtler than this interpretation would suggest, however.

There is a simple and fundamental difference between objects and ideas: objects must be produced for each time they are consumed, whereas ideas need be produced only once for all those who will use them. Consider as an object a personal computer, which is usually used by only one person at a time. Now consider a software program that makes a computer function: it can be used by a billion people at a time.

In economic terms, an "idea" would be considered a "nonrival public good."[12] "Public" indicates that several consumers can simultaneously use a particular good, such as a bridge built once for all those who wish to cross a river; "nonrival" means "not subject to overcrowding." The Austerlitz Bridge in Paris may well be jammed with traffic at 6 PM. On the other hand, Windows software will never be "overcrowded." If a billion Chinese decided to start using it tomorrow, today's users would not be limited in their own use. Indeed, the software might become more useful to them as a result of networking. It is clear that, as the market for "ideas" becomes larger, inventing new ideas will become more profitable. The same invention can be sold an infinite number of times without involving any additional production costs. (Of course, copyright laws must be strictly enforced.)

Thus, a dynamic is almost automatically set up between "globalization" (which produces a spectacular opening of the market for "ideas" produced by "symbolic analysts") and the succession of innovations and new technologies. According to this theory, we owe to world trade the formidable explosion of innovations that seems to be the trademark of contemporary capitalism. It is becoming more "profitable" than ever before to invest in the production of "ideas" in the North while leaving to the South the manufacturing of objects corresponding to these ideas. Abundant examples attest to this new division of labor: software designed in the North, computers made in the South; designs and marketing campaigns conceived in the North for shoes made in North Africa or Asia; television series produced in the North, television sets in the South.

The Fear of Inequality

Fourastié saw the "tertiarization" of the economy (a term that also aptly describes the revolution now underway) as "the Great Hope of the twentieth century," since it would allow intellectual work to replace manual labor. This development is unfolding right now. Yet we are discovering an aspect of it that Fourastié did not foresee: idea-producing economies are less egalitarian than those that manufacture objects. The propensity to exclude those who do not have ideas appears to be stronger than the propensity to exclude those who are without wealth. It is useless to look elsewhere for the reason why the world being created today is at once more unequal and more "open" than the world of the past.

World trade seems to act as the engine of unequal wealth, increasing the wages for those who have direct or indirect access to the production of ideas while allowing the jobs of the North's unskilled workers to be taken over by the South. By opening up the production of innovations, world trade probably creates incentives for long-term growth; however, by so doing it disrupts the cohesion of wage earners and causes growing tension between those who are winning and those who are losing—between, say, those who vote for the Maastricht Treaty and those who vote against it.

The fear is not that the countries of the South will sell us more than they will buy from us: if they sell us $100 worth of goods, sooner or later they will also buy $100 worth of goods from us. Nor should we fear "regressive deindustrialization": on the contrary, the countries of the South are pushing us toward industrialization that brings profits to high-added-value sectors. Finally, the fear is not that the number of jobs created will be smaller than the number of jobs destroyed: even if there were an identical number of jobs created and jobs destroyed (which is not the case), that would hardly help unskilled workers; the new jobs would not be offered to them.

What will be the destiny of the unskilled workers whose jobs are destroyed by trade? The falling demand for unskilled labor that is predicted by trade theory corresponds exactly to what happened in the 1980s in two very different institutional environments: the United States and France. In the United States, the least-skilled workers saw their wages decline by 30 percent. In France, unskilled workers saw their rate of unemployment rise dramatically—from under 3 percent in 1970 to close to 20 percent in 1990—while the unemployment rate remained more or less stable for skilled workers. Are the data sufficient to prove that trade is the cause of the new inequalities? It is one thing to point to a loss of demand for unskilled work; it is another to blame world trade for it. Most studies reject the idea that trade might be the source of new wage inequalities.[13] They point out that the percentage of workers affected by competition with poor countries is actually very small—on the order of only 2 or 3 percent of the aggregate labor force. In France, the least optimistic estimates currently give a net balance of 300,000 jobs destroyed (while unemployed workers number more than 3 million).[14] In the United States, it is estimated that the increase in imports from the South has destroyed approximately 6 percent of the unskilled jobs in the manufacturing industry. But manufacturing employs only 18 percent of the American workforce. Even if we take into account the "ripple" effect of displaced workers on the economy as a whole, these small percentages do not permit us to attribute more than one-fifth of the increase in inequalities to the competition with the South, whether it results from international trade or from immigration. In France, as it turns out, international trade actually *generates* unskilled jobs, particularly in the agriculture-and-foodstuffs sector.

On the whole, an empirical relationship between trade and inequality is weak and perhaps nonexistent in France and in the United States, and in most other rich countries—even if the qualitative relationship goes in exactly the direction predicted by the theory. It is as if globalization were just falling into place in inegalitarian societies—as if the trend toward inequality had actually come first, preparing the way for new trends in international trade.

4

The Third Industrial Revolution

Rising inequality is the key preoccupation at the end of the twentieth century. Whereas in Europe it manifests itself mainly in employment, in the United States it manifests itself entirely in wage disparity. During the 1980s the wages of young African-Americans declined by one-third. By 1990, American skilled workers had lost the gains of 30 years of prosperity: the purchasing power of their wages had returned to what it was in the early 1960s. Meanwhile, the earnings of CEOs skyrocketed from 30 to 150 times those of skilled workers. Only 20 percent of the population profited from the increase of nearly one-third in the wealth produced between 1973 and 1993; the incomes of the other 80 percent remained the same or decreased. Two-thirds of the gain in wealth experienced by American society in the 1980s fell into the hands of only 1 percent of the population.[1] Never before in the history of the industrial world had such an explosion of economic inequalities been recorded. Let us trace their development and compare them with the inequalities that result from world trade.

The Origins of Inequalities in the United States

The French have always been of the opinion that the United States is less egalitarian than their country. However, not until the 1980s did this come to be true. In the early 1970s France held the gold medal for wage disparities among rich countries, but in the next 15 years inequalities in the United States increased sharply. Now the income ratio of the richest 20 percent to the poorest 20 percent is 9:1 in the United States and 7.5:1 in France.

In 1776 the United States was a very homogeneous society of small landowners, and thus it was one of the most egalitarian countries of the time.[2] However, throughout the nineteenth century and up until World War II there was an inexorable rise in inequality, despite abrupt accordion-like shifts that often hid the trend from contemporary observers. A major accordion-like shift occurred immediately after World War II. The war had suddenly compressed the wage scale, which, to the observers' surprise, continued to narrow for the next 20 years. Owing to this so-called "Great Compression,"[3] inequality stopped increasing for a while. By 1968 the United States had returned to the income distribution it had known in 1776.

At the end of the 1960s, another drift toward inequality began. Unnoticeable during the 1970s, the rising inequality became evident in the 1980s. In the period 1979–1987, workers who had only a high school diploma lost more than 20 percent of their purchasing power. The term "working poor" was coined, referring to workers who are below the poverty line despite the fact that they are employed. In the early 1970s they accounted for 10 percent of the working population; in the early 1990s, nearly 20 percent.

What was responsible for this impoverishment? A preliminary list of suspects was quickly drawn up. In addition to globalization (examined in chapter 3), it included the transition to a service economy, immigration, the dismantling of trade unions, and deregulation, all of which have been subjects of many studies. Let me say, before briefly touching on them, that no single factor is sufficient to account for the situation at hand.

Transition to a Service Economy

The simplest of several ways of characterizing the new world of work is to speak of a service economy. By now less than 20 percent of the working population is still employed in industry, and less than 5 percent in agriculture. This means that more than three-fourths of the working population is employed in the "service sector."[4] The rise in service activities is due in part to a change in the categorization of certain tasks that used to be listed as industrial. If an accountant goes to work for himself while continuing to work for the same industrial company, he statistically reduces the percentage of "industry" jobs increases the share of "service" jobs without any changes in the actual tasks he performs. Moreover, "average" figures conceal a great degree of social heterogeneity. For instance, in France nearly 40 percent of men are still "blue-collar workers," which is obviously not without bearing on the role of industry in French society's "mental representations." But beyond that, and even more important, the idea of tertiarization masks the extraordinary degree of heterogeneity the phenomenon brings about. Whereas in industry there were many ties between blue-collar and white-collar workers, there are few economic, social, or institutional ties between a banker and a server at McDonald's.

Looming behind the issue of tertiary work are two contradictory pictures of the idea of work itself. One is a picture of twenty-first-century intellectual computer-related work (the work of Robert Reich's "symbolic analysts"); the other is an archaic picture in which "odd jobs" (i.e., domestic work and jobs as servants) are suddenly reappearing when we thought they had been abolished by industrial society. The way in which French society views the United States is a perfect example of this ambiguity: there is a fascination with the "cyberworld" and a disdain for jobs at McDonald's.[5]

Contrary to common assumptions, there was a significant *decline* in the number of domestic, cleaning, and food-service jobs in the United States during the 1980s. Two-thirds of the jobs created in the United States in the period 1990–1995 have been in sectors where wages are above average. The most dramatic increases in employment have occurred in industrial services, medical services, and financial occupations. Therefore, no trend toward task deskilling is directly associated with the tertiarization of the economy. On the contrary: tertiarization creates skilled jobs and destroys unskilled jobs.

In the case of France, the gradual disappearance of unskilled jobs is directly linked to the tertiarization the French economy experienced in the 1970s and the 1980s. This is clear from the results of a study conducted by Dominique Goux and Eric Maurin of the French National Institute of Statistics.[6] According to Goux and Maurin, the falling demand for unskilled labor in France in the 1980s is not mysterious at all: it is essentially due to the evolution of employment toward a structure that is not unlike the structure that prevailed in the United States approximately a decade earlier. This is further proof that tertiarization upgrades tasks.

Other Culprits

Several factors besides tertiarization have been implicated in the downgrading of unskilled work. Those most commonly cited are immigration, deregulation of the job market, and an uncontrollable decline in unionization.

Immigration is an area in which the social and political stakes are clearly very high. It is estimated that approximately 10 million immigrant workers, most of them unskilled, entered the US job market during the 1980s. Immigration alone provides more than 20 percent of all unskilled workers. Likewise, deregulation of the job market and the de-unionization of US workers have become significant factors, with union membership dropping approximately 10 points over the course of the 1980s. Are these factors—harmful to unskilled workers—sufficient to account for their recent impoverishment in relation to skilled workers? The answer has to be negative, since there exists yet another factor that upsets the equilibrium between skilled and unskilled workers: the rising educational level of American society.

Ignoring the changes resulting from trade, tertiarization, or immigration, we can expect the situation of one group relative to another to depend on specific demographic factors. If cleaning women are scarce, they will of course be better paid than if they were numerous. In general, if there are few unskilled workers and many skilled workers, the relative position of skilled workers is less favorable than in the opposite case, in which access to education remains in the hands of the happy few. However, the advent of mass education in the United States has been such that, according to most estimates, it is a more significant factor than any of those mentioned above. Economists who have examined factors adversely affecting unskilled workers (immigration, de-unionization, or globalization), comparing them with the adverse effects on skilled workers (represented by a rise in educational attainment in the economy and an increase in the number of educated workers), usually conclude that the skilled workers are the ones who—relative to unskilled workers—should have felt the impact of the 1960s and the 1980s. But such was not the case: better-educated workers, despite the demographic factors playing against them, actually saw their situation improve relative to that of unskilled workers.[7]

How can we account for this paradox? The economists who have brought attention to it have settled on the following explanation: If skilled labor resists the demographic factors working against it, it is simply because the demand for education is drifting upward, owing precisely to the evolution of production techniques. We saw that tertiarization functions partly in this way. But the "upgrading" of production tasks is a far greater factor in the social transformation of rich countries than the change from an industrial economy to a tertiary one. According to Goux and Maurin's study, a trend toward the transformation of the whole set of tasks can be seen within each subsector of the French economy, and in fact within each trade: "The increasing proportion of expert or managerial occupations reflects the transformations specific to each category of activities and to each sector. In industry, the increasing proportion of engineers and technicians is due mostly to internal reorganization within the various industrial subsectors. The same goes for tertiary services: the increasing proportion of expert and managerial occupations reflects the transformations specific to each category of activities in this sector."[8]

In other words, wherever we turn, and at whatever level of detail we choose to observe, labor is engaged in a process of increasing upgrading—a process that pushes aside the members of society who cannot manage to fit in. Therefore, behind the screen of globalization or tertiarization, a revolution in techniques is at the origin of the massive explosion of inequality we are witnessing today.

The Third Industrial Revolution

We fail to understand what "globalization" really means if we do not take into account the extent to which it represents but one piece (without a doubt the least fundamental so far) of a larger puzzle which we should call "the third industrial revolution." Two centuries after the first industrial revolution (which created the railroads), and one century after the second (which produced the automobile and the airplane), we are inexorably engaging in a revolution that makes each of us the immobile engine of an infinity of virtual journeys: the information revolution.

The first industrial revolution gave the economies that embraced it in the nineteenth century an annual growth rate on the order of 1 percent. The second industrial revolution has allowed a record growth rate of 2 percent per year, on average, throughout the twentieth century. I venture to say, while remaining guarded in my predictions regarding the evolution of scientific discoveries, that the third industrial revolution will allow us to do even "better."

However, what is mostly at stake in the emerging transformations is not whether the information revolution will produce a growth rate of 2, 2.5, or 3 percent per year. There can be considerable measurement errors here. It is almost as if the very idea of growth—which assumes that we know how to compare the quantity of goods produced at the beginning and at the end of a given period—vanishes when the life spans of consumer goods (televisions and automobiles, as well as computers) are constantly being shortened by product innovation. The US Department of Commerce has brought attention to the fact that US statistics in this area may have underestimated growth by a percentage point each year as a result of this problem.

At a much more fundamental level, what is at stake in the third industrial revolution is the type of organization of labor that it will generate—or, in simpler terms, the type of social cohesion that will result from it.

The O-Ring Theory

In 1993, Michael Kremer, in an attempt to represent the way in which technology makes for social reality, proposed the "O-ring theory of economic development."[9]

An O-ring is a donut-shaped rubber seal. The malfunctioning of one such seal causing the explosion of the *Challenger* space shuttle. The shuttle had cost NASA several billions of dollars, required the cooperation of several hundred teams, and combined a considerable number of components. All this work and the lives of the crew were lost because one seal failed to function properly. The lesson Kremer draws from this example is simply that, on any given assembly line, the smallest malfunction of one component puts the quality of the entire finished product at risk. As a consequence, workers who are involved in a common process must have very similar levels of competence. A team of atomic engineers cannot afford to hire a mediocre research assistant, no matter how low his wages would be. The best law firms recruit the best secretaries and pay them more than lesser firms pay their secretaries. Kremer notes that Charlie Parker and Dizzy Gillespie worked together and that Donny and Marie Osmond did too: the best work together, and so do the mediocre.

If we consider this matching of skills as a taken-for-granted phenomenon, we can imagine to what an extent the information revolution will exacerbate it. When computer technology allows production to combine much more decentralized manufacturing processes, combining components becomes much more flexible than it was during the era of mass production. A firm can now rely on a multitude of subcontractors to oversee its accounting and the design of its products. A process by which each production unit becomes a homogeneous subset of a much larger process is taking hold. Data provided by the French National Institute of Statistics give evidence of the force of this process. Between 1986 and 1992, the homogeneity of workers[10] within French companies employing more than ten individuals increased by more than 20 percent. If they were to continue at that pace (as they obviously could not), in only 20 years companies would consist of perfectly identical wage earners.

Slight differences in individual performance can consequently result in considerable differences in income, which may be incomprehensible when examined with too little hindsight.

Whoever succeeds in being hired to work on the manufacturing of the space shuttle will be paid in relation to the significance of his part in the project as a whole. Consequently, there will be a considerable difference between the salary of a computer operator who becomes part of this production process and that of an individual who must be content with an almost identical job in a supermarket chain.

In the "O-ring" world of production, negotiation does not bear as heavily on wages as does the quality of the service an individual provides. No firm wants to compromise the quality of "its" product, even if refusing to compromise means lesser earnings. The factory no longer offers the barrier of protection it did in the postwar years. Each individual who is excluded from a range of activities may have to turn to activities of lesser quality, sometimes to earn much less. The individual trajectories of careers are, thus, becoming much more volatile.[11]

The New Inequalities

A fundamental feature of the O-ring world is a decline in egalitarianism much more significant than the one brought on by the "globalization" of the economy. If international trade or immigration were the main cause of contemporary inequality, we would observe an phenomenon of inequality limited to inter-group inequalities, with less-educated workers becoming poorer and more-educated ones becoming richer. But a much more insidious force is actually at work: that of an explosion of inequality *within each socio-cultural group*. The phenomenon of inequality is occurring within each age group, each educational tier, and each sector of the economy. Just as "the whole idea of the sea is in any drop of water" (as Spinoza said), the whole idea of inequality as it has manifested itself since the early 1970s is apparent in every segment of the labor market.

In the United States, more than 60 percent of the inequality in wages can be accounted for by wage differentials among young workers, or among educated people, or among industrial workers. Even more spectacular, it would seem that more than one-third of the rise in wage disparities in the United States is attributable to the volatility of the incomes of individuals over the courses of their lives. Contemporary capitalism has therefore led to a new kind of misery by creating within each social group, and within each lifetime, tensions that were once limited to rivalry between groups. This "fractal" property of the phenomenon of inequality (in which the minutest part represents the whole) is incomprehensible to those who maintain that globalization, immigration, or any other sectoral factor is the main cause of the phenomenon of inequality. None of these things can account for the widening inequality between large occupational categories. They absolutely cannot explain why the rise in inequality is also occurring within each age group, or within each sector.

The segmentation of the labor market as represented in the O-ring theory presents a much more powerful explanatory scheme—one that reflects the replacement by the new organization of labor of modes of production inherited from the second industrial revolution. The O-ring theory also explains why "globalization," though a false explanation for the process at work, is nonetheless a good metaphor: each individual feels himself or herself to be in competition with a vaster world, even if in practice the competition remains limited. The new flexibility in the combining of tasks accounts for the much stronger segmentation in the division of labor and for the increased permeability of economies to international exchanges.

One can easily understand the new nature of capitalism by comparing the destinies of two of the best-known companies of the information revolution: Apple and Microsoft. Most observers agree that Apple, creator of the Macintosh, is more inventive than Microsoft. Not until 1995 did Microsoft develop software (Windows 95) that reached a level of user friendliness that was available on Macintoshes nearly 10 years earlier. However, Apple is now in crisis, and Microsoft is flourishing. The reason is that Apple committed a fundamental error by adopting what might be called a "protectionist" strategy: instead of specializing in the manufacture of software, the thing at which it was best, it tried to manufacture computers and printers too. Microsoft, on the other hand, chose an "open" strategy, leaving the manufacture of computers to Compaq and Dell and that of printers to Hewlett-Packard. As a result, Apple is on the brink of bankruptcy, whereas Microsoft has exceeded IBM in market capitalization. Microsoft joined the O-ring world, limiting its vulnerability by manufacturing only products within its field of expertise. Apple stayed with the concept of large factories which are judged by the complete range of their products, thus making itself vulnerable to the weakest link in the chain of which each of its products is a part.

This example leads to the heart of the process at work and allows us to grasp the essence of what we call "globalization." By creating new "matchings," the O-ring mode of production creates new pockets into which poor countries can insinuate themselves. (For example, certain computers and printers made in Asia are finding a niche in the range of products controlled by Microsoft.[12]) But these poor countries are simply filling the space opened to them by the transformation of capitalism. The internal dissolution of the large "Ford-style" factory is what makes the game between the South and the North more open. It is also what disrupts the social compromise established after World War II.

The End of Fordism

The relationship between industrial revolutions and social justice is not stable. In the nineteenth century, the first industrial revolution had thrown peasants ruined by advances in agricultural production into the cities that had in no way been prepared to receive them. This era spawned such expressions as "the great misery of the working classes" and "the workers' condition" to describe a distress that many militant followers of Marx saw as intrinsic to capitalism. A tightly interwoven set of political and social reasons that would graft themselves onto the second industrial revolution, radically changing the lives of workers, proved this analysis to be false.

As was emphatically pointed out by the French thinkers of the "regulation" school,[13] capitalism is not a mere juxtaposition of one or several industrial revolutions with the unchanging rules of a market economy; rather, it is an ensemble of production techniques and social rules, which must operate simultaneously in order for the capitalist system to function. The third industrial revolution, now underway, is wreaking havoc with the social contract that had been written over the course of the second industrial revolution—that is, all through the twentieth century. "Fordism," as this social contract is sometimes called, is dissolving. In portraying this crisis, it is crucial to carefully separate what is directly associated with the technological aspect of the current revolution from what is attributable to other social compromises. We must try to distinguish the disintegration that is due to a new industrial revolution from the disintegration that is due to political factors.

How did the now-dissolving social contract come to be known as Fordism? One day Henry Ford decided to double the wages of his workers. His well-known public explanation was that he wanted his workers to be able to buy his automobiles. This was obviously said on a whim. Purchases of cars by Ford's workers made up a negligible portion of his sales, and a much more considerable portion of his costs. However, his argument was taken seriously, and it led to many misunderstandings. In fact the reason why Ford increased his worker's wages was that he was confronted with a very high rate of worker turnover. He decided to give his workers substantial raises in order to tie them to the assembly line, and that led to the formation of a genuine working-class community within Ford's factories. The outcome of this venture was conclusive: productivity gains rapidly paid off the wage increases Henry Ford had granted, and he summed up this venture by declaring it "good business." This profitable interdependence between wages and productivity is at the heart of Fordism. Assembly-line work leads to spectacular gains in productivity, and these gains are returned in part to the workers. Instead of an inevitable relative impoverishment of the working class, as predicted by Marx, just the reverse occurred: the workers' incomes were indexed to the wealth produced.

Henry Ford was said to be concerned with whether his workers drank, but not with whether they were able to speak English, or even whether they were literate.[14] Today, however, one can no longer afford to be illiterate or not to know the language of the country one is in if one wants to be matched with an efficient production units. The end of "Fordism" marks the beginning of the unskilled laborer's true exclusion from the core of the capitalist machine.

In the early days of emerging capitalism, a growing number of vagabonds, "redundant workers," and "Old Regime" misfits formed the first ranks of those who would gradually become the wage earners of the nineteenth century.[15] In today's terms, we should ask ourselves if disaffiliation from work outside the large Fordist factory also leads to a considerable restructuring of the concept of work itself, or if it is truly a mere process of exclusion.

Along the lines of the O-ring theory, we can see that a dual process is actually at work here. If we interpret the end of the large Fordist factory as the sign of a restructuring of production centers into smaller, more "professional," and mostly much more homogeneous units, we can see that skilled workers are alienated only to a small degree. Their ties to the system remain essential, but there is much more uncertainty about the localization of those ties. An individual beginning a career at Microsoft has no idea where he will end his career; whereas someone beginning a career at Ford or Renault was practically guaranteed of ending it in the same place.

Unskilled workers suffer from a radically different kind of exclusion than skilled workers. Whatever educational efforts might be made for future generations, the destinies of low-skill workers seem to have already been determined. It is highly improbable that their alienation will serve as the premise for a new wage contract. In rich countries, low-skill workers are more likely to be the misfits of a period of transition—a period in which the demand for unskilled labor has suddenly collapsed.

5

Assortative Matching

Although the third industrial revolution is a major factor in the advent of the "new age of inequalities,"[1] it is not the only factor. The schools, the family, and even the nation are now experiencing crises, much as the Fordist factory did. The potential for social mixing sometimes offered by these institutions in the past has given way to a new segregation similar in form to that observed in the area of production. It seems that the usual loci of socialization are now becoming the centers of a process of "assortative matching"—that is, selective association among homogeneous individuals. It seems that the O-ring effect, which helped us explain why matching has to follow a principle of maximum homogeneity in the area of production, is also operating in society as a whole.

School

School plays a central role in the redistribution of opportunity. If the labor crisis were due to globalization, mass education would certainly be the ideal remedy. Let us recall the logic at work: trade with poor countries destroys low-skill jobs and creates high-skill jobs. Therefore, in the absence of changes in the population, there is suddenly a surplus of unskilled workers and a scarcity of skilled workers. A much more effective remedy for this disequilibrium than protectionism would, then, be to raise the educational level of the population, since a sufficient increase in skilled labor might even out the proportions of skilled and unskilled workers.

Unfortunately, however, we must moderate the ardor of those who would like to see education as the universal remedy in the struggle against inequalities. As a matter of fact, some economists do not hesitate to attribute the origins of the new age of inequality to mass education itself.[2] This argument may appear paradoxical, but it actually corresponds to a number of insights into the loss of interest in unskilled labor.

In a society in which there are few skilled workers and many unskilled workers, the best use of the former is to give them tasks that involve the latter as subordinates. It is, after all, a key concept of the Fordist factory to create strongly hierarchical production centers in which highly skilled engineers run factories employing unskilled workers. However, a rising skill endowment of the population modifies the logic of this matching. When the number of available skilled workers increases, another logic can actually begin operating: since they now constitute a larger community, skilled workers are encouraged to group together within much more homogeneous production units. From a world in which the factory played a role in social mixing and internally redistributed the wealth produced, society moves *as a result of education* to an inegalitarian mode of production in which more educated workers stay among themselves, subcontracting to others the "lowly" tasks that they do not want to perform. Instead of simply reflecting the information revolution, this new logic of "assortative matching" will in fact be the logical response of society to the new composition of its labor force.

The conclusions thus reached go strongly against insights originating in naive theories of globalization. According to such theories, *partially* educating the population is sufficient to offset the *partial* effect of job cutbacks, since, thanks to the education of others, an unskilled worker can always profit from the decongestion of the market in which he is looking for work. In the standard theory, the worker who remains unskilled is *helped* by the upgrading of his neighbor, even if he himself does not profit directly from it. In the new theories we are proposing here, the exact reverse occurs. A worker who does not participate in the task-upgrading efforts of society as a whole is left behind. Thus, from the point of view of the "classical" theories of globalization, setting a goal of having 80 percent of the population receive high school diplomas is excellent for everyone, including the remaining 20 percent. But if we believe in the theory of assortative matching, it is *disastrous* for the remaining 20 percent: in a world in which 80 percent of the population can read, remaining illiterate is an insurmountable obstacle for the other 20 percent. If "literacy" today means "speaking English" or "understanding computers," we have come to the crux of the modern issue of exclusion. The argument obviously does not imply that the march toward mass education should be slowed down. However, it helps us understand why, in the meantime, education threatens to amplify exclusion.

"Assortative matching" is already at work within the educational system. France's Third Republic school system, which put socially heterogeneous schoolchildren side by side in the classroom, can be interpreted as the logical organization for a school system in which there are few teachers. As soon as the numbers of students and teachers reached critical mass, parents adopted a more selective educational strategy for their children: they formed tighter communities that segmented education in a much more exclusive manner than was the case in the early days of the public schools. Now the "good" schools become the "best" because they can take advantage of a larger pool of students and teachers; the average schools follow suit, and so on.

As the French sociologist Agnès van Zanten notes, "these selection strategies are used mostly by middle-class families, in particular professional families which, even if they lack the necessary means to live near the best schools, can avail themselves of the services, know-how, time, and social networks required to decode and manipulate the complex selection and matching systems."[3] Parents are not the only conspirators in these selective strategies, however. The schools contribute to it as well, sometimes unconsciously. In Van Zanten's words, "splitting the student body into relatively homogeneous groups—making use of such pedagogical tools as the creation of programs based on student aptitudes or options—has been, for school principals and teachers, one of the best ways of dealing with difficulties in teaching and the discipline problems due to increasing numbers of students and growing internal heterogeneity." She concludes: "When faced with the implicit or explicit threat that parents in more privileged circumstances . . . will turn to other schools, middle and high schools (and sometimes even elementary schools) in less privileged neighborhoods are more and more tempted to reconstruct subtle hierarchies between social classes. These hierarchies take the shape of a range of options, from prestigious 'European programs' to 'music' or 'theater' classes." This says it all. In the image of the Fordist factory, public schools are feeling the paradoxical effect of mass education: they are becoming more segmented, thus contributing to the emergence of new inequalities.

The Family

It may seem strange, or even naive, to put the family on the list of institutions suffering from the new inequality. Let us separate form and content.

In terms of form, nothing more closely resembles the expressions used to describe the employment crisis than the expressions used to refer to the "dysfunction" of the family. Economists who specialize in the study of labor refer to the rate of worker turnover in companies as the "separation rate"; just as I have done, they speak of "matching" when describing the logic of what should be called the "marriage" of a company and an employee. Theories of the family actually preceded the type of analysis I have presented to account for the functioning of the job market. The new theories of segmentation in the job market are in fact directly inspired by models developed by Gary Becker, an American economist, in his formalization of an "economic approach to the family."[4] In order to show the analogy between these two different worlds, I will briefly present Becker's thesis.

Becker's ambitious goal was to "export" the methods of economic analysis to the most intimate behaviors of human life—specifically, the behaviors of individuals within families. The methods of economic analysis can actually be summarized in terms of a small number of concepts.

An economist who examines a problem first concerns himself with supply and demand factors. It is not even necessary, if we want to understand the "terms of exchange" between two factors, to impute explicit prices to the factors. In applying these ideas to family relationships, an economist who notes that there are more women than men living in cities (and the reverse in the countryside) will be able to conclude, irrespective of "price," that the urban marriage "markets" will be more favorable to men—for example, that at the very least a bachelor will marry more quickly in a city than in the countryside. The analysis could, if necessary, be refined in terms of socio-occupational or age groups.

The second notion used by economists is the substitutability or complementarity of two entities on the market. A factor of production or a consumer good is said to substitute for another if the scarcity of one can be balanced with the abundance of the other. For instance, tea and coffee are substitutable commodities. If there is no coffee but there is tea, the world will not stop turning, and consumers will switch from coffee to tea without too much difficulty. In short, the scarcity of coffee will increase the consumption of tea, if only partially. Conversely, coffee and sugar are complementary factors: if sugar becomes unavailable, the consumption of coffee will suffer, since some coffee drinkers need sugar in order to appreciate coffee.[5]

In the area of marital relations, what is relevant here is obviously not the complementarity of men and women; it is the nature of the traits that should be shared by a couple. If the main objective of marrying is the sharing of financial wealth, a substitutable commodity, then the richer one of the spouses is the less necessary it will be for the other to be rich. If, on the other hand, the main objective is to find a spouse who has the same aesthetic tastes as oneself, then the traits that the pair will seek to share are complementary: as the consumption of coffee is reinforced by the consumption of sugar, so is one partner's pleasure in going to a concert reinforced by the pleasure that the other finds in it.

According to Becker, if love is separated from material well-being and marriage becomes primarily a matter of taste, "marriage markets" will operate through assortative matching—that is, couples will be more homogeneous than in the past, each individual looking for a spouse who shares his or her tastes and who resembles him- or herself. When the formation of couples functions on the basis of love rather than money, it does not become any more egalitarian. Attempting to share a spouse's tastes rather than his or her wealth is actually more selective, since no compensatory phenomenon can intervene. The world in which a ruined aristocrat could marry a wealthy bourgeoise, or a talented young man could marry his master's daughter, is giving way to a world in which individuals who share the same values tend to group together. By some estimates, half of the rise in income inequalities among households in the United States may be explained by this increasing propensity for assortative mating.

But in fact it is mostly through changes in the divorce rate that the strategies of assortative matching manifest themselves. According to Becker's analysis, these changes are related to a rise in earnings, particularly those of women. Once a woman can have access to a salary that permits her to become autonomous, nothing can stand in the way, as it could in the past, of her reconsidering a marriage that does not (be it from the woman's or the man's perspective) satisfy the ideal of shared happiness on which it was founded. The labor market offers opportunities for a new freedom that makes separation much less problematic from the material point of view, therefore permitting "tastes" to express themselves even more freely throughout the course of her life.

The parallel transformations of couples' lives and of the functioning of the labor market can be deduced from this analysis. Once the occupational destinies of individuals become a crucial variable contributing to the definition of their identities, we can equally understand that the vagaries of the job market affecting people translate irremediably into a threat to the married couple. If one partner succeeds in his or her professional life and the other does not, despite almost identical starting conditions, the couple will be threatened by the new asymmetry that will then have set in. If the contemporary world must be characterized by rising inequalities in destinies, given identical points of departure (this has been called the "rise in intra-group inequalities'), then it is certainly in order to expect divorce rates to increase too.

Sociologists approach the issue of divorce in a broader way, but they reach a similar conclusion: the relationship in a couple is now based on a contract between two people who aspire to be equal, and it is therefore in the very nature of the contract that it can be freely voided as soon as one of the two parties is no longer happy with it. As François de Singly notes: "Under the social pressure to achieve individual self-fulfillment, modern couples must follow the rhythm of identity changes in each partner. Mobility is obligatory: it is assured by a new definition of the functions assumed by each of the partners, engendering separation, preceding the eventual formation of other couples."[6] According to Singly, the apparent dysfunctions of marital life can actually be interpreted as the outcome of a Western dynamic that, according to Norbert Elias, forcefully replaces such social norms as moral rules and politeness with "internal principles of regulation of which the sole legitimacy is the 'self'."[7]

Becker's explanation regarding the new role of the labor market and Singly's wider-ranging explanation regarding contemporary individualism reinforce each other. The egalitarian sentiment upon which contemporary couples are based is a factor in the breakdown of hierarchical societies—a breakdown which Louis Dumont clearly showed to be intimately linked to the emergence of a market economy.[8] This may be the meeting place for two men who happen to have the same last name: just as René Dumont denounces the effects of African hierarchical systems on the exploitation of women, Louis Dumont shows how the emergence of contemporary *Homo aequalis* cannot be dissociated from the increasingly powerful market economy.

Therefore, it is to be expected that the breakdown of hierarchical systems on which marriage used to be based is causing a rise in the divorce rate in the rich countries. However, the new propensity toward what Irène Théry calls "unmarriage" are complex: "It upsets ways of life, the freedom gained transforming and inevitably multiplying sources of conflict. Everyone is now threatened by what he or she claims as their most precious possession, namely a private life completed as an individual and open itinerary."[9] This transformation of the family is perfect testimony to the modern individual's difficulty in being. One wants to be free to "divorce" one's family or his work; however, as soon as one finds oneself thrown into a world in which divorce is becoming the rule, one feels dizzy. As Pascal Bruckner suggests, democratic man seeks to rid himself of traditions, but as soon as he succeeds in doing so he is nostalgic about them.[10]

We can understand the philosophical aspect of this process on the basis of the traditional opposition between the Age of Enlightenment and Romanticism. As Robert Legros describes it in his book *L'Idée d'Humanité*, the Enlightenment and Romanticism both started from the same "modern" postulate: there does not exist a "human nature" in the sense in which an "animal nature" might exist; there are only social artifacts. But two radically different series of implications emerged from this same point of departure. For the Enlightenment, man became authentically himself by "breaking away" from cultural and religious traditions (which he could wrongly consider as "natural" to himself). Man's search for "autonomy" in relation to the society that is his home thus became man's characteristic. For the Romanticists, in contrast, humanity existed only in and as a result of the specific civilizations, religions, and languages it had created. The Enlightenment's project of tearing man away from them was dehumanizing: "autonomy" only led to the search for satisfaction of the "needs," and these artificial needs, which man persuaded himself were "natural," actually lowered man to the level of an animal.

Romanticism is a critique of the Enlightenment, but the Age of Enlightenment can also be seen as an anticipated critique of Romanticism. To accept (along with the Romanticists) that civilizations are "natural" to man is to hide from ourselves that they do not just spring up on their own. To accept their authority in advance is to deny man's freedom regarding his creations. But the Romanticists' critique of the Enlightenment is equally valid: autonomy, when it becomes an end in itself, is certainly "dehumanizing."

This opposition, which corresponds perfectly to the transformations experienced by contemporary capitalism, sharpens two contradictory tendencies in modern man: the desire to share the new page of the history of humanity represented by "globalization" and the fear that this process will be "dehumanizing" and will create a world too vast for human communities.

The Nation

The nation is also subject to a process of "assortative matching." In the nineteenth century it was thought that large countries were worth more than small ones because a large country had a large domestic market and therefore a stronger economy.

The formation of Germany and that of Italy were based on a model for which the United States still serves as the point of reference today. Militant US protectionism enabled US companies to put in place impressive economies of scale, and thus to become full partners in the gigantism of emerging capitalism. The resulting model includes a large market, a federal state with enough power to protect the domestic market, and a common currency[11] to unite the domestic market. We readily recognize this model as the foundation of efforts toward national unity in the nineteenth century, as well as of today's efforts toward the construction of Europe.

However, the idea that a large domestic market is better than a small one is breaking down now that the world market offers each country the largest possible market. A small country is no longer obligated to forfeit the benefits of a large market in order to form a political entity. As a consequence, the prosperity of large countries now presents a shattered image, and in the 1990s many small countries were able to emerge. Most of them resulted from the breakup of the Soviet Union and the fall of the Berlin Wall, but the separatist tendencies within the richest countries (Italy, Belgium, and Spain, for instance) show the strength of the trend. The successes of Singapore and Hong Kong alone would suffice to invalidate the idea that a large domestic market is a necessary condition for growth.

As a consequence, political economists are now proposing new arguments *against* large countries.[12] The essential argument in this regard relates to the heterogeneity of their populations, which forces substantial redistribution and which overburdens a large country's economy with debt and inflation. Small countries, being more homogeneous, are not subject to this risk. Czechoslovakia, by forfeiting its national unity, freed itself from the political burden of having to force Czechs and

Slovaks to live together. On the other hand, Belgium, by artificially maintaining a combined Walloon-Flemish community, is burdening itself with a costly redistributive system; as a result, its public debt is one of the highest among the OECD countries—just behind that of Italy (which owes its debt to a heterogeneity between its northern and southern regions that, although not of a cultural nature, is very pronounced).

The radically new idea developed in this literature is, thus, that economic integration reduces the necessary size of political communities. This idea is based on the simple assumption that globalization makes it less necessary to maintain large countries for the benefit of their large domestic markets. It is therefore not surprising that local and regional politics are gaining in significance while "national" politics is experiencing a crisis that is often interpreted as a rejection of plain and simple politics. Thus, it is not the least of globalization's paradoxes that it has consequences at the political level rather than at the economic level, not so much making countries too small in relation to the world market as making them too vast to take on the fundamental role assigned to them: marking the boundaries of democracy.

One World?

The French director Roger Planchon was recently interviewed about the role of theater in a society flooded with images from all over the world. Planchon responded that, in his opinion, the role of theater is reinforced by globalization, because only theater manages to maintain human proximity between a piece of work and its spectators.

Planchon's response could also be applied to many other areas of social life. Societies' sudden opening to a vaster world

gives rise, as we have seen, to a demand for closer social relationships. It is as if economic life and political life were following opposite paths. One is opening; the other is closing.

The narrowing of political life poses two serious problems
that will no doubt set the stage for crises and transformations
to come. First, the search for a new "international cohesion"
will encounter difficulties. Unless we accept the naive liberal hypothesis according to which the market is self-sufficient, we
need to reflect on the elementary principles that can organize
the contemporary world, whether they have to do with trade or
with the humanitarian principles that will have to govern (for
example) an international policy of public health. Stateless by
nature, but also deprived of states because their political space
has been reduced, the world is stumbling blindly into an unprecedented adventure whose outcome even the shrewdest
among those who hold an "end of history" position should not
be able to predict.

It is in this framework that Europe may play a fundamental
role—in the search for cohesion in the area of global equilibrium, and in the support it can bring to the formation of the
rules that globalization will require. If, on the other hand,
Europe thinks that it can use economic globalization as an argument for intervention in the "internal" cohesion of European
countries, it is headed for a rude awakening. That would be
tantamount to reinforcing the authority of parents in the selection of spouses as a way to fight divorce, without understanding that "political" legitimacies, far from becoming broader, are
in fact diminishing as a result of the opening of exchanges.

6

Unemployment and Exclusion

If the "dysfunctions" of the factory, of the family, or of the country can be interpreted as a modality of the inequality crisis, can we understand Europe's experience of the employment crisis in these terms? European countries do not seem to have registered as spectacular a rise in wage disparities as the United States. Most European countries went through the 1970s without changes in the salary scale, and it was not until the very late 1980s that rising wage disparities began to manifest themselves in a still imperceptible way.[1] But whereas in the United States unemployment has remained fairly flat since 1973, Europe has known an upheaval that is at the core of a seemingly insurmountable increase in mass unemployment that resembles a crisis of civilization.

There is actually an almost perfect correspondence between the manner in which Americans represent the crisis of their industrial society in terms of wage disparities and the manner in which Europeans account for it in terms of unemployment. As Paul Krugman puts it, "moneyless America" and "jobless Europe" represent two facets of a single phenomenon. Various societies have reacted to the phenomenon with various institutions, which have pushed them in directions that seem to be opposed but are actually very similar in one sense: each society is threatened with new forms of segregation.

Mass Unemployment

Europeans discovered unemployment quite suddenly. For instance, in France unemployment stood at 3 percent of the working population in 1973. By 1976 it had surpassed 6 percent. In 1996, it amounted to 12 percent. Driven by uncontrollable forces, unemployment has brought down all the governments that, one after another, had made its resorption the objective of their economic policy. In retrospect, however, we can say that the rise in unemployment during the 1970s is much less surprising than it seemed at first. France was simply coming to the end of an exceptional period: the postwar "golden age" simply marked a period of Europe's catching up with the United States. Immediately after World War II, per-capita income in France amounted to 40 percent of per-capita income in the United States; by 1975 the percentage had risen to 80. Allowing for possible measurement errors, we can say that France had become as rich as the United States by the mid 1970s. It was unavoidable that France would experience slower growth again—either rates corresponding to its own secular average (2.1 percent per year in the twentieth century) or rates equal to those experienced by the United States during the "golden age" (2.5 percent per year).[2]

When analyzing changes in the unemployment rate in France from the 1960s to the 1980s, one can either uphold the view that the rate rose sharply after the mid 1970s or draw up a graph of a "step function" showing unemployment to have increased from a low rate (2 percent) in the 1960s to a higher but stable rate (9–10 percent) in the 1980s. The logical nature of this "step function" can easily be explained on the basis of the slowdown in growth. All other things being equal, there is less hiring in times of 2.5 percent growth than in times of 5 percent growth, because the efforts needed to seek out, train, and equip a newly hired worker are not as well rewarded in the case of weak growth as in the case of strong growth. When economic growth slows down, it is unavoidable that the demand for jobs and for equipment will undergo a long-term slowdown. And it is possible to prove a strong parallel between these two variables.

If the growth rate could again be what it was in the 1960s, there is no question that unemployment be significantly lower than it is today. It is tempting to believe, on the basis of this common-sense argument, that only a policy encouraging strong growth can resolve the unemployment problem. But that argument is thwarted by the unfortunate fact that growth cannot be decreed, since it depends (as we saw in chapter 2 in relation to poor countries) on the accumulation of capital and on technological progress. And technological progress has slowed considerably. It provided a spontaneous "bonus" of 3 percent per year to growth in France during the "golden age," but since the mid 1970s this "bonus" has been under 1 percent per year. Technological progress was spectacular in the 1960s because European countries could freely take advantage of American innovations. Today it has returned to the pace experienced by countries that have reached the boundaries of progress; it is slower and more uncertain, and its destructive forces are often without clear direction.

However, it would be wrong to think that the countries that have been most successful at resorbing unemployment are the ones in which growth has been the strongest. From 1973 to 1993 the United States had an average growth rate that was exactly the same as that of France: 2.3 percent. Since 1973 unemployment has quadrupled in France, whereas it has roughly leveled off in the United States. This difference is, therefore, due to factors other than growth.

A comparison of unemployment in France and the United States is informative. At the peak of its economic cycle, in the late 1980s, France had an unemployment rate on the order of 9 percent. At the low point of its cycle, in the mid 1990s, it had an unemployment rate on the order of 12 percent. In the case of the United States, we would have to compare the following figures: In 1997, at a high point of its economic cycle, the United States had an unemployment rate of 5 percent; at the lowest point of the cycle, in the early 1980s, the rate was about 8 percent. We must take these fluctuations into account when comparing unemployment in France and the United States. For a rigorous analysis, we must compare either the high points with the high points (the 5 percent rate in the United States with the 9 percent rate in France) or the low points with the low points (the 8 percent rate in the United States with the 12 percent rate in France).

If we push it further, the comparison leads to the following conclusions: On the one hand, France could choose to bring its unemployment rate from 12 percent down to 9 percent through a reversal in the cycle. (The debate this opens up is at the core of economic policy.) On the other hand, if we simply focus on comparing the high points in the cycle—9 percent for France and 5 percent for the United States—we need to ask what the reasons are for the difference and how the situation could be remedied.

Thousands of articles have been written on this theme. I will summarize them briefly without attempting to highlight the various points of view represented.[3]

One general conclusion is that no single primary reason can be found; rather, we are dealing with multiple, interrelated determinants. For example it can be said that France's *salaire minimum interprofessionel croissable* (index-linked minimum wage) discourages employment and may account for one percentage point of the unemployment rate; that unemployment benefits, which are more generous in France than in the United States, account for approximately half a percentage point; that firing costs and various laws regulating overtime and the like may account for a one-percentage point difference. The residual gap can be attributed to the use of different statistical methods: in the United States the jobless are often counted as non-working individuals, since a number of them do not find it worthwhile to claim low unemployment benefits.[4] (Obviously there is room for debate about the relative importance of these factors; I have tried to present the general consensus.)

To conclude the debate with the above data would be to fail to highlight an essential aspect of unemployment. Just as "average" figures for wages in the United States would fail to account for the substantial rise in inequality accompanying them, average figures for unemployment detract from the most important issues: the inequalities and the potential for exclusion that result from it. Rather than attempt to refine our analysis of the determinants of average rates, let us turn to a detailed examination of unemployment.

The Falling Demand for Unskilled Labor

The key to European unemployment is actually the same as the key to American wage inequalities. Beyond the inevitable effects of a slowdown in growth, the employment crisis should first be seen as reflecting a new decline in the demand for unskilled labor.

An examination of the rising unemployment rate in France from the early 1970s to the late 1980s reveals a substantial increase in the asymmetry between the destinies of workers according to their levels of education. In the early 1970s, the unemployment rate for skilled workers (2.5 percent) was quite close to that for unskilled workers (3.5 percent). The employment "crisis," which was exacerbated over the course of the 1970s and 1980s, was in reality nothing but the crisis of unskilled labor: by 1990 the rate of unemployment for skilled workers was 4.5 percent, whereas that of unskilled workers was nearly 20 percent. As measured by unemployment rates, the crisis therefore appears to have affected only unskilled workers; in Europe, as in the United States, they were the victims of a seemingly universal decline in the demand for unskilled labor. This crisis manifested itself in pay cuts in the United States, whereas in Europe it manifested itself in a decline in employment.

There are at least two reasons why joblessness would affect unskilled workers more than skilled workers. The first is an obvious asymmetry: a skilled worker can always accept unskilled work, whereas the converse is not true. A recent high school graduate can sell pizza during the summer, but a recent high school dropout cannot teach math classes while waiting for stable employment. This leads straight to the second reason, which goes to the heart of a fundamental question about education: Has it become an instrument for creating better jobs, or does it simply serve as a mechanism for promoting some individuals over the heads of others in a job market that has become intangible? Each of these two extreme viewpoints has its defenders in the economic literature. In the mid 1970s, Michael Spence published an essay upholding the viewpoint that education functions only as a "signal" for employers during the hiring process.[5] According to this theory, the particular subject matter taught in school has absolutely no intrinsic value. All that counts is the individual's aptitude for learning and for reacting to competitive circumstances, so it does not matter in the least whether we teach humanities or mathematics.

Studies conducted by education experts often confirm the value of this hypothesis. For instance, in a paper titled "Do educational degrees become devalued as they multiply?"[6] Christian Baudelot and Michel Glaude report results that partially validate Spence's approach. They find the salary structure to be remarkably stable as long as salaries are correlated with the hierarchy of degrees rather than with the absolute number of years of schooling. Students who are among the most educated 10 percent tend to keep their salary positions relative to the 10 percent who follow, and so on. As the number of people holding a high school diploma increases, the value of the diploma decreases, but not the position of those who maintain—relative to the mean—the same educational differential that used to be represented by a high school diploma. Given the correspondence between salary hierarchies and educational hierarchies, we are forced to recognize that a mechanism such as that described by Spence probably is operating.

To lengthen the duration of studies remains a rational strategy for individual students but would be absurd and deplorable for society as a whole. If deviation from the mean is all that counts in the long run, any efforts made by society to increase the mean would be in vain.

At the international level, educational attainment is clearly a determining factor of prosperity—as is evidenced by the Tigers. At the domestic level, however, education clearly functions as an instrument of differentiation of the labor force as much as it functions as an element of qualification.

Yet there is a striking fundamental difference between France and the United States: when unemployed, an unskilled American worker does not spend any more time trying to find a new job than a skilled worker. The jobs to which he has access are continuously declining in quality, as we saw earlier; however, unemployment does not result in exclusion from the world of work. In France, an uneducated unemployed person spends more than twice as much time looking for a job as a skilled worker. Here is the crux of the difference: in the United States unemployment is an "ordinary" state that one can rapidly change, whereas in France it is a poverty trap from which it is difficult to escape.

Why does unemployment function as a machine of exclusion in France, while it is but a transitory point (experienced by a large number of workers) in the United States? In other words, why does the phenomenon of inequality affect the number of available jobs in France, whereas in the United States it is reflected in the wage gap? We cannot answer this question without first examining laissez-faire theories regarding the relationship between wages and employment, and Keynesian critiques of those theories.

Laissez-Faire and Keynesianism

In the laissez-faire view of the economy, employment disequilibria are spontaneously resorbed on the labor "market." Unemployed job seekers exert downward pressure on wages until each of them has found a job. The idea that there necessarily exists an "equilibrium" wage for which all those wishing to be hired will be hired is not based on empirical evidence; rather, it results from a cynical notion: for rock-bottom wages, everyone will find a job. Thus, there necessarily exists a (possibly very low) wage at which everyone will manage to be hired. Whether low wages are socially satisfactory is an altogether different issue which must be solved by society's political, redistributive choices.

The critique of the idea that labor demand results exclusively from wage negotiations is at the core of Keynes's work. His demonstration is fairly straightforward. In the case of unemployment, Keynes is the first to admit that wages will decline, reflecting the reduced bargaining power of wage earners. But since prices are themselves indexed to wages, they will also decline. Unemployment will therefore most likely induce a decline in nominal wages (expressed in dollars), but there is no guarantee that it will produce a decline in *real* wages (that is to say, wages earned after adjustment for inflation). Therefore, the question—to be determined by the general economic situation—is whether prices will decline more rapidly (or will go up more slowly) than wages. If the general economic situation is favorable, prices will indeed increase more quickly than wages and real wages will decline, favoring hiring; in a recessionary period, real wages will increase despite the decrease in nominal wages. We need only remember what occurred in the 1930s to be convinced. In the United States, nominal wages declined by more than one-third during the Depression, but prices declined more rapidly than wages. The fact that real wages increased during this period was evidently not due to wage earners, but rather to the crisis itself. Keynes therefore concludes that wages do not determine employment; rather, employment (industry's decision to hire as a result of the economic situation) determines (real) wages.

What, then, determines employment and the economic situation? Quite simply, changes in industry's outlets. As

Keynes notes, in addition to having the necessary production equipment, firms need to find outlets in which to sell their products in order to decide to produce and hire. It is not this consideration in itself that separates Keynesians from the classic or "neo-classical" thinkers; rather, it is the analysis of the manner in which these outlets are found. An economist who follows Smith's or Ricardo's model will claim that a firm seeking outlets will always find them if it lowers its prices sufficiently. In the search for new clients, it will unknowingly upgrade the purchasing power of wage earners (and of rentiers, according to Keynes).

For Keynesians this sequence does not lead to the expected equilibrium, since a firm that lacks outlets will not simply try to lower its prices. Rather, it will first dismiss workers, and, as a result, no matter how much prices are lowered, there will never be enough outlets to create "full employment," simply because the jobless do not have any purchasing power. Thus, in the Keynesian perspective, everything that can contribute to a slowdown of the layoff process is good from the viewpoint of the functioning of society. Likewise, whatever can stand in the way of wage deflation will necessarily be a step in the right direction, since it will avert a downward spiral toward underemployment. Finally, whatever efforts can be made to maintain the purchasing power of workers—whether they are employed or not—will also be very positive.

Keynes was the avatar of a new age in political economy—an age in which the issue of the supply of goods would become non-essential in relation to the demand for them. Making consumers (especially jobless consumers) solvent rather than making producers solvent, and realizing that gaining in wealth equals spending: such was the glorious future of capitalism as promised by Keynes.

The Phillips Curve

If wage negotiations are not the direct cause of unemployment, exactly what role do they play? They simply determine inflation. Post-Keynesian economists lent substance to this idea by readily accepting the Phillips curve,[7] which represents the relationship between inflation and unemployment as follows: when unemployment is too high, wages and prices decrease; when it is too low, they increase.

When the growth of the 1960s was at its peak, "full employment" indeed led to the wage explosion forecast by Phillips's correlation. The logic of the Phillips curve—that with almost full employment comes the threat of inflation—found general acceptance.

The logic of the Phillips curve would have predicted (on the basis of symmetry) that the slowdown in growth and the rise in unemployment that affected the European countries in the 1970s would result in downward pressure on wages. But things happened differently. All through the ten years that followed the first (1973) oil-price shock, the share of wages in value added was on a continuous rise, going from 63 to 69 percent in France, while unemployment doubled. "Stagflation" (a combination of unemployment and inflation), the scourge of the 1970s, was not explicable in terms of the Phillips curve, according to which we should have one evil or the other, but not the two evils simultaneously.

How is it that wage earners' bargaining power was not adversely affected by the rising rate of unemployment? Various explanations have been proposed over the years. An early one, based on the rigidity of declining real wages, turned out to be unsatisfactory. According to this explanation, the evolution of the purchasing power of wages would conform to the logic of the Phillips curve, with unemployment adversely affecting wage growth. However, workers are much more "obstinate" when they need to accept a decline in their purchasing power. Wage earners refused to absorb the quadrupling of oil prices through wage reductions, and, in spite of rising unemployment, they made firms responsible for the necessary adjustments.[8] The problem with this explanation is as follows: The cost of oil amounted to only 3 percent of France's gross domestic product. Since economic growth itself amounted to 3 percent yearly at that time, it should not have taken very long to cancel out the effects of the oil crisis *if real wages had remained stable.* The question was therefore promptly reworded as follows: Why did wages continue to grow despite the increase in unemployment?

Insiders and Outsiders

Economic theory had to resort to new paradigms to answer this question. The most convincing can be summarized as follows: Wage negotiations are not affected by the jobless, for the simple reason that wages are negotiated by those who have jobs and are therefore determined so as to protect the jobs of those who are employed, rather than to make job seekers employable. And protecting one's own job means setting one's own wages on the basis of the evolution of one's own productivity, rather than on the basis of the potential productivity of the jobless.

This so-called insider-outsider theory provides an explanation of why wages continue to grow despite the increase in unemployment: For an insider, the only risk is that he might lose his job. As soon as unemployment levels off or begins to decrease, an insider can feel free of that risk, and can try without fear to obtain wage increases based on the evolution of his own productivity. This particular theory abandons the notion of an "equilibrium" unemployment rate (a certain level of unemployment beyond which wages decline and below which they regain ground). Each level, as it is reached over time, serves as a point of reference for the future.

It is easy to apply the insider-outsider theory to economic developments in France. P. A. Muet, for instance, remarks that wages started increasing when unemployment reached 3 percent in the period 1966–1973, when it reached 6 percent in 1977, and when it reached 9 percent in 1989.[9] He estimates that, overall, the minimum unemployment rate that serves as a trigger for wage negotiations is determined in a proportion of 80 percent by the phenomenon of hysteresis predicted by the insider-outsider theory, and only in a proportion of 20 percent by a phenomenon of return to a fixed level.

This attractive theory seems to correspond to the evolution of the wage share during the 1980s and 1990s. Accepting the theory has radical implications, however.

First, any attempt to fight inflation through a rise in unemployment is both efficient in the short run (since a rise in unemployment will set back wage increases) and dangerously injurious in the long run: whatever level it reaches, unemployment will later resist efforts to bring it down.[10] Furthermore, the insider-outsider theory implies that it is useless to attempt to reduce the cost of labor by lowering payroll taxes, since the decrease would be absorbed by wage earners who already have jobs.

In brief, the insider-outsider theory forces us to renounce the idea that fiscal policies might help to fight unemployment. It also leaves practically no hope for the fight against unemployment other than an open and radical fight against entitlements (that is, the whole panoply of regulations) which permit insiders to protect themselves against outsiders, their rivals.

Unemployment and Exclusion

Let us now return to the concrete functioning of the labor market. What form does the barrier between insiders and outsiders take in France, and why does it not appear in the same form in the United States?

We cannot clearly understand the essential difference between unemployment in France and in the United States by examining only *rates* of unemployment, which give a distorted picture of the phenomenon at work because they encapsulate in a single number a situation that is actually has two dimensions: the rate at which jobs are destroyed (called the *separation rate*) and the amount of time it takes for the jobless to find jobs.

The difference between France and the United States does not lie so much in the number of jobless individuals (in proportion to the total population) as in the different paces at which jobs are lost and found in the two countries. Each month, close to 2 percent of the working population in the United States becomes unemployed; the corresponding figure for France is 0.4 percent. But an American will, on the average, remain jobless for less than 3 months; his French counterpart will spend more than a year looking for a job. In other words, *unemployment is much more frequent and much less prolonged in the United States than in France.*

One need not examine the data in much detail to understand why unemployment is not a factor of exclusion in the United States: a period of joblessness is an ordinary aspect of the life of an American worker, whereas it is still a rare event in the life of a French worker (despite France's higher rate of unemployment). Over four consecutive years, 85 percent of a cohort of French workers never experience joblessness.

Since it occurs rarely, unemployment in France quickly becomes a stigma for those who do not manage to avoid it—they are truly considered outcasts. France creates and destroys more than 4 million jobs per year. Relative to the total population, this is very close to the corresponding number for the United States. However, there is a considerable difference: in the United States, a majority of workers who change jobs go through a period of unemployment. In France, more than half of the workers who change jobs go directly from one job to another. Out of 4 million jobs created every year, fewer than a million are offered to the jobless. Two million jobs go to currently employed workers, 1 million to workers who had not previously been counted as jobless.

In this light, we can see to what extent any fear of having jobs destroyed by global trade simply misses the point. Trade with poor countries may have resulted in 300,000 job losses in France—a ridiculously low number in relation to the job destruction due to "ordinary" capitalism. At stake is not so much the rate of job destruction as the way in which French society concentrates the effects of job creation and job destruction.

In the United States, jobs are "open" to "all," jobless or employed; in France they are concentrated in a much more restricted hard core of insiders. Why? The most direct answer is that in the United States employers are unafraid to hire because it is just as easy for them to lay off. In France, the relationship between a company and its employees is not of the same nature. Irrespective of legislation on layoff procedures, it is governed by what Philippe d'Iribarne convincingly describes as guidelines based on a "code of honor."[11] In France a worker cannot be summarily dismissed, whereas in the United States an employer would not hesitate to lay off an employee who was late for work two days in a row. D'Iribarne accounts for this difference in attitude in terms of the history of France: anything that evokes the idea that a social relationship revives Old Regime hierarchical relationships is banished. In the United

States, democratic sentiments are at the very foundation of society. As Tocqueville noted, an American servant is never in a servile position; he is in a freely entered contractual relationship. He can leave with no advance notice, and likewise he can be dismissed overnight.

This comparison leads to the following considerations. French firms behave in a way that simultaneously results in many fewer dismissals and many fewer hires—in both cases, in proportion of the labor force, one-fifth as many as in the United States. This prudent attitude regarding jobs necessarily leads to longer periods of joblessness—a phenomenon that has deep roots. In 1968, when the level of unemployment in France was negligible (much lower than in the United States), a jobless individual already had to wait 9 months to find a job. The crisis that followed the oil shock prolonged this wait by 4 months and thus increased the unemployment rate, but the radical difference with the United States was already part of social reality in France well before the unemployment rate exploded.[12]

In practice, it is obviously very difficult to separate what is due to historical traditions or to what d'Iribarne called the "code of honor" from what is due to the pressure of certain specific factors (firing costs, labor contracts, etc.). However, we must look at the overall picture. Even when growth rates are the same, it is much more difficult for the French labor market to integrate the jobless than it is for the American labor market. If the market cannot easily absorb those who are excluded from prosperity, why can a higher degree of solidarity not exist to ward off the phenomenon of exclusion to which French society exposes the most vulnerable segments of its population? In other words, why does politics seem to find it as difficult to integrate the outsiders as the economy does?

7

The Poverty of Politics

Three distinct stages can be distinguished in political economy
(a field which I consider to comprise both the theory and the
practice of relationships between the economic and political
spheres). The first stage is that of mercantilism, in which urban
elites exploit rural areas and corrupt society in the name of industrialization. At this stage, one could say, politics absorbs
economics. The second stage is that of economic liberalism,
whose main point is to abolish mercantilist regulations so that
society is "governed" by the market—more by default than by
design—and the economic sphere absorbs the political sphere.
At the risk of being accused of caricature, one might say that
this is the kind of political economy operating in certain Asian
countries today. The third stage of political economy is that of
Keynesianism, in which democracies try to regain control of
their economies. Under Keynesianism, because of unemployment, government is once again playing a central role in the
regulation of the economy, and it is rediscovering some of the
prerogatives and motivations of mercantilist states. (It is interesting to note that some of Keynes's writings aim at rehabilitat-
ing mercantilist thinking.)

The brand of Keynesianism that shaped the policy making of
rich countries after World War II is now in crisis. It is very

tempting to blame globalization for the current problems in this area—as it was to blame it for problems in other spheres discussed in this book. Here again, however, the crisis of Keynesianism is due much more to society's internal transformations than to external influences. The real problem is that the macroeconomic regulation proposed by Keynes cannot easily keep up with internal developments in divided societies.

The Crisis of Policy Making

The failure of economic policies is often justified in terms of the idea that the crisis of Keynesianism is among the evil consequences of globalization. According to this analysis, government's diminishing control must be attributed to the damage caused by the commercial and financial opening of economies.

In the 1950s and the 1960s, when governments were trying to stabilize their economies on the basis of Keynesian principles, they interpreted the Keynesian message as an incentive to use public deficits to regulate demand—that is to say, as the appropriate instrument for avoiding recession. In case of recession, governments promptly used public spending to increase purchasing power and thus to revive economic activity and boost growth. However, two constraints—one internal and one external—restrict the operation of such policy making.

The internal constraint lies in the fear of inflation, as indicated by the Phillips Curve: with excessive boosting of economic activity comes the risk that companies will react by raising their prices rather than by increasing production. The external constraint lies in the fear of deficit in the balance of payments: spending too much in proportion to production levels may create a situation in which foreign merchandise must be imported, thus creating disequilibrium with the rest of the world.

Today these two constraints are often brought up by those who are pleading for cooperative economic policies at the European level. An autonomous European central bank responsible for price stability would make it possible for European countries to adopt more aggressive budgetary policies. Likewise, concerted action through budgetary policies at the European level would result in considerable alleviation of the external constraint. Since the bulk of European countries' trade is conducted with other European countries, a concerted economic revival would increase imports *and* exports; as a result, the balance of payments of each European country would be much less likely be out of control.

There is no question that these excellent arguments weigh in favor of policy coordination in Europe. Europe suffers from a handicap in its macroeconomic management relative to the United States, which can manage its monetary and budgetary policies in a relatively coordinated manner. However, there is a great deal of hypocrisy in this debate: neither inflation nor the balance of payments is actually the major constraint on the operation of "autonomous" economic policies. One reason why the debate over fiscal policy is so ambiguous in Europe today is that budgetary policy is suffering from a disease that was practically unknown in the 1950s and the 1960s: the crisis of public finances, which inexorably restricts the scope of government action.

Throughout the postwar years, public debt had very little bearing on decisions made by governments, for a simple reason: growth was strong, interest rates were low (or even negative), and as a consequence of these two combined factors any deficit experienced during a slump hardly affected government finances. Today, the cost of interest on the public debt represents the main item of government spending in most OECD countries, since debt increases in proportion to interest rates (which are now high) while a government's fiscal revenues increase only in proportion to the now-slow pace of economic growth. A government can obviously take measures to stabilize its budget in order to "improve the economic situation." But postponing the resolution of its deficit problem puts a country's solvency at risk. Italy, Belgium, Ireland, and Greece have lost all ability to use the public deficit as an instrument to counter unfavorable economic conditions. In each of these countries the amount of public debt has made it extremely costly to revive the economy through measures based on budget deficits.

As a result, governments are reduced to taking budgetary measures that vaguely correspond to the economic situation: in periods of weak growth, the decrease in fiscal revenues worsens the budget deficit; in periods of stronger growth, attempts are made to consolidate the budget balance. Such ad hoc measures are short lived. If by any chance the recession lingers for a while in one country, as was the case in Sweden in the early 1990s, the extent of the deficit may very quickly lead to a reconsideration of the measures put in place. Today, this new-found prudence is hardly due to the fear of inflation or of external deficit; it is due entirely to the risk of seeing public debt impose an inevitable burden on government revenue.

External Constraints: A Poor Argument

This crisis of public finances is often ignored by those who underestimate the current risk of insolvency in the most indebted countries, as well as by those who regard it as simply a consequence of globalization. There is no question that financial globalization creates a subtle dialectic between dependence on and support of public finances. Thanks to financial globalization, governments have recourse to international financial markets and can more easily finance their deficits. By so doing, they become progressively vulnerable to the positions of external investors: whenever there is a lack of confidence on Wall Street or in Zurich, the financial crisis threatens to reach debtor countries. This dialectic follows the usual pattern of tensions induced by strategies of opening: opportunities and dependence.

However, the problem is different in the case of pay-as-you-go social security (prevalent today in most of Europe), where the creditors and the debtors are both domestic agents: the working population and the non-working population. This interface is not governed by any "Zurich gnome." The question before us is this: Will pensioners be able to recover, from the present working population and (especially) from the future one, what is (implicitly) due them? There is no place for "financial globalization" in this issue: the debt that might be repudiated (the payment of pensions) is not mediated by financial markets, and it would be of no consequence to financial markets if working individuals were to decide, in the year 2015 or later, that pensioners will not receive what they regard as due them.

During the "bleak" period 1980–1995, France experienced average annual growth of 2 percent. This figure, which may seem insignificant to some, actually represents an increase of close to one-third in national production—and, incidentally, it is equivalent to the rate of increase experienced by France throughout the eighteenth century. However, this growth rate only produced frustrations and anxieties, partly because it was below the expectations that had gradually developed during the "golden age," but partly because the apportioning of this growth was almost entirely absorbed by the aging of the active population. During this period, pensioners' income increased by close to 4 percent per year, whereas the net income of working individuals increased by only 0.5 percent per year.[1] It is obviously absurd and demagogic to blame globalization for the difficulties rich countries have in resolving their internal conflicts in the area of redistribution.

The crisis of the French welfare state must be understood in the context of the time period in which it originated. In France, pensions themselves are the result of a social contract drawn up in the 1950s and the 1960s, when it seemed that a growth rate of 5 percent per year would last forever and when there were only 300,000 students enrolled in France's universities (compared to more than 2 million today). From this perspective, speaking of "defending social security" without being more precise as to what that means amounts to defending a welfare state whose choices no longer correspond to contemporary inequalities.

A number of phenomena indicate that the solidarities put in place by the French welfare state now function in a cruelly discontinuous manner. For instance, the newly prosperous 60–74 age group is surrounded by age groups in desperate situations. Those over 75 constitute the group with the highest level of poverty. If the welfare state is supposed to be a solidarity state, how can such a lack of balance in individual destinies be accepted? The absence of solidarity also affects the "younger old" (those 55–64 years old), who feel the full impact of the crisis in the French labor market. Contrary to common assumptions, these people—and not the young—are the ones hit hardest by the unemployment crisis. An individual over 50 who loses his job waits 6 months longer than one under 50 and suffers a loss of purchasing power of nearly 50 percent.

The cruel differences in the destinies of French individuals in rather similar social categories is also illustrated by the functioning of the index-linked minimum wage (SMIC). This instrument efficiently reinforces the bargaining power of the most vulnerable employed workers, who in its absence would probably be the equivalent of the "working poor" whose numbers multiplied in the United States during the 1980s. At the same time, the SMIC completely abandons to their fate those for whom it becomes a barrier to employment. There are no provisions or remedies for those whose productivity is inferior to the level dictated by the SMIC. More precise, they cannot be "assisted" by society until they have been relegated to the category of the long-term jobless.

The Recurrent Nature of Poverty

At a time when poverty is back on the scene in countries once perceived as rich, the long-standing debate on the best way to ward it off is also making a comeback. Must the poor be put into modern reincarnations of "charity hospitals," such as France's temporary public-service jobs? Or, to the contrary, must charity be abolished in order to force the poor to search the market for a job of any kind, which would ensure reentry into society? This dilemma, which is almost a replica of the one that preceded the abolition of Elizabethan laws concerning the poor (and led to the repeal of laws "favorable" to the poor) in Great Britain, seems to ignore the power of the present welfare state.

At the dawn of capitalism, when a debate on poverty was raging, the only fiscal leverage available to governments consisted of the few resources they had inherited from Old Regime governments: taxes on wigs, windows, salt, and so on. Today, half of the wealth produced is subject to government appropriation or redistribution. How could such great amounts of money not solve the problem of poverty if our societies were to make a political commitment to do so? We can no longer ignore the existence of internal diversity in our societies when addressing this issue. The idea of public power's working for the common good is fading. It is essential, if we wish to pursue the debate, that a distinction be made between the "technical" issue of the battle against poverty and the "political" issues that this battle faces in contemporary democracies.

To begin with the "technical" aspect of the debate: What resources could governments mobilize if battling poverty were their most central political objective?

If we are willing to recognize that we are past the Fordist era, in which wealth was simultaneously produced and redistributed, we are forced to conclude that government subsidies must now be directed to individuals rather than to firms. Under François Mitterand, the French left celebrated its reconciliation with companies at the worst possible time, when they were abandoning their redistributive function and becoming prey to unequal enrichment themselves. Consequently, the subsidies received by French firms throughout the 1980s were granted in vain. It does not help to lament that firms no longer play the role of "citizen firms," and it is just as absurd to try to force them to do so; at the same time, it is useless to devise policies under the assumption that they are still playing such a role.

Subsidizing individuals must, therefore, become the cornerstone of the welfare state. We must, however, avoid targeting the most vulnerable segments of the population for subsidies, even if such policies are adopted for the good of the people. Policies that are too narrowly defined can be detrimental to those for whom they were designed. Dominique Schnapper summarizes the drama of policies aimed at fighting exclusion aptly: "Social policy disqualifies those to whom it lends support by giving them the status of assisted. . . . How can we escape a dilemma which has plagued every policy meant to combat poverty in every society known to history; how can we alleviate poverty and exclusion without labeling individuals as poor/ excluded and consequently making it difficult for them to escape their condition?"[2]

Many examples attest to the aforementioned problem. For instance, although the creation of Priority Education Zones (ZEPs) in France has stopped the worsening of educational results of children in disadvantaged neighborhoods, families of higher social standing have decided to leave those neighborhoods because of "the perceived stigma of the ZEP label."[3] Likewise, Denis Fougère came to the following conclusion regarding the French labor market: "Given the functioning of the labor market, it is important for government to avoid focusing too much on groups which are eligible for some types of special assistance: they may become even more stigmatized in the eyes of future employers. . . ."[4]

The only way to solve this contradiction is to break away from the logic of targeted subsidies and come up with broader ideas, whether they be in the area of education, of suburbia, or of work. This simple statement indicates the magnitude of the task. The fight against poverty cannot be regarded as separate from the functioning of society as a whole. It cannot be "regulated" by "punctual" measures that isolate the poor in their ghettos. On the contrary, it should be directed by a constant search for open bridges between the center of the system and its periphery.

This is not the place for an inventory of the measures to be taken in order to deal with poverty in schools, in communities, or in families; this discussion is limited to the issue of remuneration for work. The simplest remedy for alleviating poverty in rich countries is known to many, even though it has often been left out of the debate—by liberals because it was proposed by a "conservative" economist, by conservatives because they are awed by the extent of the resources such a project would entail, and by both camps because of the rethinking it would require. This remedy, known as the "negative income tax," amounts to guaranteeing each working-age individual a minimum income whether the individual finds a job or not.[5]

The fundamental advantage of this simple proposition is to relieve society of having to designate an individual as a minimum wage earner, since each individual receives a minimum income which he is no longer forced to give up upon finding a job.

The debate might be simplified and concretized as follows: Some would limit the minimum income to, say, $200 per month. At the other extreme, some would say that this income should constitute a veritable living wage (comparable, say, to the minimum wage). For the latter, the living wage is the actualization of the society of abundance promised by Keynes, and production is secondary to income.[6]

But what is at stake in the fight against contemporary inequality is of another nature. We must avoid giving to the most disadvantaged individuals subsidies that will lock them into poverty traps from which they will be unable to escape (owing to the psychological consequences of subsidization and to the stigma attached to it in the eyes of others). From this point of view, what we really need is an intermediate level—say, about half the minimum wage—available to everyone. The objective is to find a happy medium that would help the most disadvantaged without isolating them in new ghettos.

Should this minimum income replace the minimum wage? If we maintain the idea that the exclusion-versus-protection dilemma should be avoided, other intermediate solutions can be found. For instance, in order to combat poverty in the working population, the Clinton administration has developed an efficient instrument—the Earned Income Tax Credit—that allows workers themselves to be subsidized rather than the firms that hire them: each time a worker at the bottom of the social ladder earns $100, the US government gives him up to $40 in some cases.[7] The advantages of this measure are clear: it allows society to remedy wage inequality without artificially creating a wall between those who are employable at the minimum wage and those who are not. It shows that we can correct inequalities generated by the market without being forced to hinder the mechanisms of its functioning. In summary, it proves the social efficiency of a fiscal system not governed by political considerations. The only question here is: Just how far will society go in the area of solidarity with the most disadvantaged workers?

Obsolete Political Attitudes

Our failure to make full use of the mechanisms that would extricate us from the dilemma of "market" versus "charity" is due less to uncertainty about efficiency than to a new kind of distrust of redistribution. It is obvious that lowering taxes is becoming a much more popular electoral argument than increasing redistribution. What is at stake in the new political economy now taking shape is an assessment of this question: What political alliances can bond societies around a politically acceptable distribution system?

We need to know at the outset if fighting inequality actually corresponds to the political agenda of the median voter. The issue is subtler, however: Can a majority of individuals simultaneously fear globalization and worry that politics will fail to cancel out its negative consequences? These two apprehensions seem to be in contradiction. If a majority of voters share a fear of globalization, why do they also have doubts about their own capacity to cancel its effects? Why could this same majority not decide to engage simultaneously in unequal economics and redistributive politics? Let us follow the analysis of Raquel Fernandez and Dani Rodrik.[8]

Let us consider a society made up of 100 people who start out by earning $1 per year each in a perfectly egalitarian society that produces $100 each year. Let us now interpret "globalization" (in the general sense of trade and industrial revolution) as a reform that allows 60 individuals to double their income but also halves the income of the other 40. Here globalization increases inequality but still enriches society as a whole, since the aggregate income rises from 100 before globalization to 140 after it ($60 \times 2 + 40 \times 0.5 = 140$). A society not bound by its fiscal system would choose to engage in globalization: in order for everyone to be satisfied, an individuals whose income rose from $1 to $2 would simply need to agree to compensate the "losers" by at least 50 cents.

But that does not solve the problem: even if a society were committed ex ante to compensate the losers, nothing would force the gainers to actually do it ex post. A consequence of globalization in a society is to create a rift between the rich and the poor. As long as those who benefit from this transformation constitute the majority, they are in no way politically obligated to compensate the losers. The democratic consensus will exclude the "losers" from prosperity—not only as a result of the laws of the market, but also because their effects can no longer be canceled by the laws of politics.

This argument can be refined. If society did not know in advance the identity of the 60 individuals who will benefit from trade, will it choose to vote in favor of a transformation that generates such inequalities? If each voter is a "gambler," each may believe that the odds of success are greater than the risk of loss and therefore vote for globalization. But suppose that globalization is not "blind," and that the identities of 49 of its 60 beneficiaries are known in advance. The 51 individuals who do not know how globalization will affect them are now confronted with a very different choice: they know that only 11 of them will gain. Even if they are "gamblers," there is no longer any hesitation: the 51 who are uncertain about their futures will vote against globalization. The "veil of ignorance" that obscures their future will stand in the way of voting for the change.

What is fascinating about this example is that it facilitates an understanding of the political irreversibility of certain social transformations. In the example we have studied, a society that has chosen the path of unequal wealth persists in it, whatever its hesitations may have been in the past. France can be said to be watching the United States from the other side of this Rubicon of inequality, doubting (perhaps rightly) its own political capacity to reverse the flow of inequalities once it has taken that direction.

If we interpret European unemployment as one of the manifestations of this new inequality, we nevertheless see that European societies have probably already come to the other side of the river. Pierre Rosanvallon attributes the crisis of the French welfare state to the lifting of the "veil of ignorance" that covered French society right after World War II.[9] Today, by contrast, everyone has become cognizant of his or her position in society, and it has become much more difficult to redistribute wealth.

The New Individualism

Should we conclude that a revealed majority of French voters are satisfied with the present redistributive system? Are the 60 percent who are gainers abandoning the rest of society to whatever fate may befall it, purely on the basis of ballot counts? This is too mechanical a conclusion: individuals' attitudes toward poverty are not dictated solely by their own social positions. Thomas Piketty's studies provide evidence that voters are much more likely to vote in accordance with their own representations of the world than to vote with their strictly economic interests. As Piketty demonstrated, voting patterns are often determined much less by a voter's own social position than by that of the voter's parents.[10]

Let me illustrate this argument with a more concrete example, using the results of an experiment in applied psychology that will help us understand such attitudes toward redistribution.[11] Each of ten children was asked to make a drawing. When the drawings were finished, the organizer of the experiment picked one of them at random, announced that it was the nicest, and explained that its creator deserved a $20 bill as a reward. Once the prize was given to the child, however, the teacher whispered in that child's ear that one of the other nine children was very ill and could be helped by the $20 bill. In 90 percent of the cases, the child gave the money to his schoolmate. The outcome of this experiment was then compared to another in which, instead of waiting until the drawings were finished to reveal that the nicest drawing would receive a prize, the teacher announced right from the start that the nicest drawing would be rewarded with a $20 bill. Once the drawings were finished and the nicest (chosen at random as in the first experiment) was rewarded, the teacher told the same story about the ill schoolmate. This time, the winner's answer was radically different: in 90 percent of the cases, that child kept the money.

This experiment attests to a simple and profound reality: altruism and concern for the other are not intrinsic to human nature; rather, they depend on each individual's representation of the social world to which he or she belongs. The first child received an unexpected reward and consequently felt generous toward another child; the second child saw the $20 bill as a reward earned by his effort and acted selfishly

This anecdote can lead to various conclusions. One of them underscores a difference in attitude that has been emerging in Europe since the end of the postwar "golden age": as long as one earns more than one thought one would (as was the case in the postwar years), one feels generous and works toward social protection "for all." Conversely, in a time when one must constantly lower one's expectations, one becomes more individualistic, fighting for one's "own" pension fund without taking into account the situation of others.

This experiment allows us to grasp the difference in attitude between France and the United States. When interviewed about the causes of professional success, the French respond "networks, luck"; the Americans respond "ambition, work." A French person who has succeeded is like the first child in the experiment above: he believes in his luck. The American is like the second child: he believes in the results of his efforts—even though in practice the social reality is actually very similar on both sides of the Atlantic (since social mobility patterns are comparable in France and the United States, contrary to common assumptions). The Americanization of society so feared by the French may be operating in the area of individuals' representations of society, in a more "concerned" attitude in the workplace, in a new picture of the efforts to be made in order to ensure one's professional success.

The Fourth Stage of Political Economy

Paradoxically, the fear that economics will produce an inegalitarian, "dehumanizing" society accompanies a new form of individualism whose political effect is to reinforce—rather than lessen—the centrifugal forces operating in the area of production. Wavering between economic and political considerations is engendering what might be called the "fourth stage of political economy"—a stage in which economics and politics scrutinize each other and neither of them can any longer dominate the other. In view of the current rates of mandatory deductions from wages (close to 50 percent in France), it could be said that politics and economics are now equals: politics is losing the dominance vested in it by Keynesianism, but at the same time the "market" does not succeed in imposing its law.

Politics itself is becoming a "market." Politicians "sell" programs—and, like good salesmen, they target the most "solvent" part of the market: the central segment of the middle class, whose moods and expectations are closely watched. In the United States, there are promises of tax cuts to compensate the decline in wages; in France, there are vague promises of preserving "entitlements." In each case, the same kind of equilibrium is reached: one that makes governments less and less solvent and less able to fight poverty. Consequently, there are limited choices in fighting poverty: it must be fought either through the market (as in the United States) or through charity (as in France).

Keynes was concerned about the insolvency of the jobless, and he demonstrated that unemployment was due to their inability to consume. Today, we need to denounce their political insolvency. The welfare state, which generously accords its protection to society as a whole, is being replaced by a state burdened with debts—a state whose only means of curbing the growing demands placed on it lies in making threats that it is in danger of becoming insolvent itself. This strategy, which is perhaps the only one available, is distressing. We cannot with impunity turn ungovernability into a principle of government. Neither macroeconomic regulation nor the fight against inequality will be possible until government regains control of public spending.

The difficulties governments are experiencing in trying to keep control of the evolution underway are due to many demographic and social factors. But the strictly "political" issue, defined here as the ability to draw up a plan that can replace the current system, is also of prime importance. In fact, the debate appears to be caught in the vise of an absurd alternative: either maintain or abolish the current system. Such an alternative results in part from the original debate about the welfare state: Should we count on the market to govern society, or should we set up complementary institutions that will limit its scope? Obviously this is still an issue of paramount importance; however, it should not be confused with another issue: how to decide on the proper form for the expression of social rights. Transforming the welfare state does not mean abandoning a critical examination of the market in which it originated; rather, it means modifying a structure that was conceived within the framework of the era of Fordism—that of the second industrial revolution—in order to adapt it to the inequality engendered by the third industrial revolution.

Conclusion

As rich countries are beset by doubts about their future, poor countries fit perfectly the role of barbarians whose horses paw the ground at the gates of Rome. However, waiting for the barbarians is like waiting for Godot: they will not come. The rich countries, by convincing themselves that they are besieged by an external threat, have become blind to transformations that they initiated. In their search for external scapegoats, they have drifted away from the search for the "common good" and renounced the "sweet warmth of wealth and peace."

Not only are analyses that attribute the misfortunes of the democracies to the countries of the South mistaken; they also push the democracies in wrong directions. Two of the errors are particularly significant. One is the idea that successfully confronting international competition requires that the welfare state be weakened. The other, which often results from the first, is that the democracies must "internationalize" political life in order to "manage" globalization. These ideas, often expressed in good faith, push democracies in exactly the wrong direction.

Rather than needing less protection, rich countries need the kind of protection that can be modified so as to adapt to the new kind of inequality that is emerging. The crisis of the welfare state is not governed by financial globalization; it is the crisis of a system that was designed at a time when the risk of unemployment was practically nil, life expectancy remained short in relation to retirement age, and growth was so strong that no one could doubt that the contributions of the working population would always suffice to finance the pensions of the retired. Adapting the welfare state to the new world of contemporary inequalities obeys an internal logic in which globalization counts very little.

It is also wrong to think that the political arena itself must be "globalized" in order to ward off the crisis. The pioneers of the idea of a European Union are attempting to prove that forming a "United States of Europe" will help to resolve the difficulties experienced by European countries. Their misfortune is that (to parody a well-known formula) they have succeeded rather than failed in their desire to copy the United States. The rejection of "Washington," which saturates the rhetoric of political campaigns in the United States, is incomprehensible to a European who attempts to interpret it in terms of an equivalent rejection of "Paris" or of "London." However, it becomes totally transparent as soon as Washington is compared to "Brussels" or the European Union. Such rejection is intelligible only to those who understand the local, almost intimate nature of the current crisis. Thinking that the crisis is global does not help to resolve the loss of legitimacy of public action, and in Europe it creates an atmosphere of discredit that distracts Europe from its essential tasks.

Those who use globalization as a point of departure for understanding the present crisis are making an error in reasoning that obviously carries with it a risk of the greatest significance: it might favor the rise of a new form of protectionism that would destroy the expectations of poor countries. For those countries, world trade is not simply a figure of speech; it is a promised end to what may be regarded as a parenthesis in the history of mankind: two centuries during which the countries of the world allowed gaps in prosperity and power to widen in a manner unprecedented in the history of the world. The great hope of the twenty-first century may first consist of bridging the gap between countries—a reasonable hope, as we have seen. It may also include the hope that Western countries will start thinking in political terms again, at a time when economics has ceased to strengthen social bonds; unfortunately, this is an area in which our optimism must be more guarded.

Epilogue
The World's Odyssey

Economists examining the patterns of "convergence" between poor countries and rich countries have been quick to point out the importance of investment and educational attainment as conditions for "catching up."[1] However, another simple but significant point they have made is that a poor country has the best chances of converging with rich countries when its geographical neighbors are doing the same. Such a concept (known as the theory of "Convergence Clubs") may at first seem like a truism: it should not come as a surprise that an economy will grow faster if it is in a "supportive environment." But there is more to it: the spillover phenomenon does not result from commercial interaction; rather, it seems to originate in a deeper process that can best be described as mimetism—what the economist Paul Romer calls a pooling of the same "ideas," whether they be social or technological in nature.[2]

This mimetism should not come as a surprise. It is a powerful engine of the history of mankind for both individuals and countries. Once agriculture was discovered, approximately 12,000 years ago, it did not take long for the discovery to spread to the rest of the world. Prehistorians estimate that the Neolithic revolution progressed at a rate of 5 kilometers per year. Their examination of this process led to another discovery:

the Neolithic revolution, which originated on the biblical shores of the Jordan, carried with it the deities known in that region. For instance, the unusual pairing of a goddess with a bull—an early expression of Neolithic deities—is attested in regions that, not long before, apparently had not yet adopted them.

This somewhat anecdotal information brings us back, however, to the central questions of the present day: Do Western countries, when exporting machines and modes of production, also export their "deities" and their values? And in which order are these exchanges made: machines first and values next, or vice versa? In other words, is adherence to capitalist ideas a prerequisite for an industrial revolution? These difficult questions may be easier to tackle if we examine the surprisingly precise answers provided by prehistorians.

Yesterday

What was the chain of events during the Neolithic revolution? Jacques Cauvin[3] cites a commonly held view (developed by Gordon Childe) that attributes the discovery of agriculture to an exogenous cause: a major climatic change that led to a sudden destruction of game animals and thus forced humans to find other ways of providing for themselves—a need that led to the discovery of agriculture. As a consequence of this experience, humans transformed their way of life, becoming sedentary and discovering new deities that fitted their new environment. But this explanation has now been rejected on the basis of precise carbon dating. It appears that sedentary life *preceded* the invention of agriculture. Jericho, the first city in human history, existed before the first crops of wheat. This discovery is sufficient evidence in itself that game animals were abundant enough for humans to become sedentary: as Cauvin states, "the switch to agriculture was not at first a reaction to scarcity conditions."[4] The diminishing number of living sites at the end of the tenth century attests to social rather than demographic factors. "It is not a coincidence," Cauvin notes, "that the expansion of Jericho was marked by architectural activities of a new, communal type, which imply cooperation regarding community oriented tasks."[5]

Belief in deities also seems to predate the Neolithic period. This appears to be more difficult to prove: how can the anteriority of a belief be demonstrated? Prehistorians establish it by noting, first, that the custom of burying the dead predates the Neolithic period by centuries. They then note that just before the Neolithic period humans gradually ceased to represent only animals, introducing figures that look very much like representations of deities. These figures were most often of women, and very rarely of animals. The only animal figure was that of a bull. Since we know that humans did not yet hunt wild oxen at the time (they hunted gazelles), the bull probably carried new symbolic value. Later, the two figures were combined, the woman represented as giving birth to the bull. This is the image that was carried along by the Neolithic revolution in the early days of its diffusion to other societies.

Such is Cauvin's summary of the transformation. Humans, no longer captives of nature, took on a new role of created beings—a role that enabled them to become creators. "The new gap which established itself between gods and humans . . . must have completely modified the representation that the human mind had [of its environment]; it must also have led to new initiatives by unleashing, so to speak, the energy necessary to carry them out, as the compensatory consequence of a newly felt existential malaise. Neolithic societies, up until then spectators of the natural cycles of reproduction of the living world, then took the liberty to intervene as active producers. . . . It is as if 'religion' had first developed—at a level which was not directly utilitarian—a sort of 'transcendental logic' which later operated on the real world by giving it new meanings within a system of modified relationships."[6]

These spectacular findings go to the heart of the question. Did the "spirit of capitalism" precede capitalism? To convince oneself of the answer, one would only have to note that Adam Smith's book *The Wealth of Nations* was written before the beginning of the industrial revolution—a revolution that Smith himself apparently was unable to imagine. We may likewise soon discover that the current wave of globalization is spreading production techniques as much as the (individualist? democratic?) values in which they are grounded. If such a form of globalization is underway, must we also fear a uniformization of the world? Probably not, as is attested by the diversity of ancient civilizations born of the Neolithic period. As Fernand Braudel stated: "Assuming that all civilizations of the world succeed, sooner or later, in uniformizing their ordinary techniques, and through these techniques some of their ways of life, the fact remains that, for a long time to come, we will still be confronted with differentiated civilizations. For a long time to come, the word 'civilization' will exist both in the singular and the plural."[7]

Today

A simple inventory of the world's present inequalities shows strikingly how much more must be done to eliminate differences in wealth. A Western traveler visiting the metropolises of developing countries is immediately struck by persistent contrasts. Tourists visiting Egypt may be just as impressed by the overpopulated and unkempt alleys the base of the Sphinx as they are by the pyramids. The *terra incognitae* described by Jean-Christophe Ruffin are there to remind us of just how much of the territory is still undeveloped.

Such images are at once real and deceptive. They are real because they remind Europeans and Americans that they are—for example—much richer than Egyptians. The difference corresponds approximately to the difference in the standard of living between the wealthiest 1 percent and the poorest 1 percent of the population in rich countries. But this gap is deceptive. If Egypt could grow at the rate forecast for Asia (7.5 percent per year), it would take less than 15 years to eliminate half of the gap between it and Europe; as a result, around 2025 Egypt would have made up three-fourths of the gap. Obviously a similar narrowing of the gap cannot reasonably be expected by any poor individual living in a rich country, or for his children or even his grandchildren.

For a long time, the comparisons of income levels between rich and poor countries have underestimated, sometimes to a considerable extent, the income of poor countries. For example, the task of a hairdresser working in a developing country is fundamentally no different from that of a hairdresser in a rich country. But, as Jean Fourastié notes, "a hairdresser in New York who does not really work more than a barber in India should be paid as much as a steel factory worker in Chicago."[8] For a given task, an Egyptian barber will also make less money than a Parisian barber—even if they both do the same work— simply because his clients are poor, and his own alternatives are not as promising.

Let us now reverse the argument: If a haircut costs one-thirtieth as much in Cairo as in Paris, it follows that in reality the purchasing power of someone living in Cairo is greater than it seems. He earns less (in dollars), but a substantial number of local goods (haircuts, various other services, rent, and so on) are less expensive. To establish a reasonable comparison between the income of poor countries and that of rich countries, we must therefore reevaluate—sometimes to a considerable extent—all activities that are not tied to world trade: when calculating the income of poor countries, we must include the additional amount corresponding to the cheaper local goods.

After such reevaluation, we are left with a radically different picture of wealth in the world. According to traditional methods of calculation, rich countries—which account for a little less than 20 percent of the world's population—earn close to 80 percent of the world's wealth. According to the new method of calculation, rich countries and poor countries each earn approximately half of the total wealth.

It is a coincidence that this partition is not very different from what can be observed within rich countries. For example, in the United States and in Europe, the wealthiest 20 percent of individuals earn between 40 and 50 percent of the aggregate wealth; consequently, as in the poor countries, the remaining 80 percent must be satisfied with the other half of the wealth. Given these figures, we can predict that inequalities *within* countries are most likely more acute than inequalities in the world. What we might call "the great hope of the twenty-first century," namely a convergence of incomes throughout the world, is already underway.

From One Protectionism to Another

Is it possible that, in their effort to fight domestic inequality, rich countries might stop the reduction of worldwide inequality by forestalling the advent of truly global trade? Protectionism is a long-standing tradition in rich countries. In the nineteenth century, going beyond mercantilism, most European countries and the United States defended the virtues of protectionism, contrary to Ricardian principles. Making an exception for Great Britain, one can therefore agree with Paul Bairoch that "a protectionist customs system was the rule for all countries undergoing development during the eighteenth and nineteenth centuries."[9] The theory of comparative advantage and its deindustrializing consequences for Southern countries (as described above) easily account for the apprehensions of other European countries, which are eager to catch up with Great Britain's industrialization.

However, protectionism is not a "natural" theory that can reconcile the interests of the "nation" with those of the rest of the world, any more than free trade is. Like free trade, it privileges some groups over others, and the conflict between groups can become extremely violent. The American Civil War, although it was waged in the name of the abolition of slavery, is good evidence that the stakes can be high. The economic aspect of the Civil War was very simple indeed: the Southern states, which exported agricultural products to Great Britain, fully profited from free trade. They located solvent markets in Great Britain, and they were able to import the manufactured goods they needed at low prices. In contrast, the Northern states wanted to keep the agricultural products of the South for their own consumption, and wished to protect their newly emerging industrial potential from British competition. Therefore, for exactly symmetrical reasons, the North practiced protectionism as much as the South practiced free trade. After 5 years, the North won the war, thus proving that in the military area industrial societies have a definite advantage which has obvious links to European countries' preference for protectionism.

Although the theory of comparative advantage is sufficient to prove (contrary to the British experience) that protectionism aids the industrialization of countries for which it is *not* a comparative advantage, that theory would obviously fall short of showing how resorting to protectionism is a good thing "for everyone." Thus, the protectionist camp has to find other arguments to prove its point. This need can be met by the theory of "infant industries," which, as its name suggests, asserts that, like a child, an industry still in its infancy needs to be protected from outside aggression before it can gain real comparative advantage in relation to other countries. This theory, further developed by Frederick List (a German), allows at a general level for justification of the protection accorded to young industries; at a specific level, it served as a foundation for the Zollverein, a customs union that was established by Prussia in the nineteenth century. What was clearly at stake in this union, according to List, was the establishment of a sufficiently protected group that could develop a "German" industry sheltered from British competition and would allow agricultural resources to be retained rather than exported.

In a somewhat similar fashion, the construction of the European Union has traced a circle around the countries adhering to it. In the aftermath of World War II, the European Union has led to a successful opening of trade in countries whose external relationships remain strongly marked by the brand of their previous colonial ties. As in the case of other factors, this period of opening was hidden from view during the postwar "golden age"; it is therefore difficult to say exactly to what extent it has contributed to the exceptional success of the postwar years, but obviously the tremendous disillusionment that Europe is experiencing today is attributable to the European plan's dependence on a model which its proponents have (at least implicitly) characterized as able to provide "protection" against the excesses of free trade.

North-South and North-North Trade

Here it may be useful to specify a fundamental difference between intra-European trade (or, more generally, trade between rich countries) and North-South trade. Trade between France and Italy, for example, is "intra-sector" trade, which means that there is an exchange of nearly identical products (which are categorized within the same production sectors): France sells Renaults and imports Fiats. Such trade forces producers to align their costs, since any long-term difference in price would be subject to sanction by the customers. But when a Southern country sells a product to a Northern one, it forces the Northern country to completely abandon production of that product. Trade then becomes *inter*-sector: for example, Northern countries import textiles and export software. It is in this arena of North-South trade that comparative advantage takes on the radical sense that Smith or Ricardo gave it: those who specialize in a certain category of products count on others for products they no longer manufacture themselves. As a consequence, in the case of North-South trade, *there no longer is cost alignment*: when our trade involves products that we no longer manufacture ourselves, we must hope—and no longer fear—that the imported products will be an inexpensive as they can be. The cheaper imported textile products or televisions are, the greater the purchasing power of individuals in the importing countries. The lower the price of Asian textiles, the more money a wage earner in France will make, *regardless of the sector in which he works*.

The strength of this argument is acknowledged not only by consumers but also by producers. Robert Reich notes that in the case of the United States—and we may add in the case of Europe as well—economic nationalism (that is, the temptation to fall back onto the domestic market) soon appeared counterproductive to producers who had been its main proponents at the outset.[10] For example, when the American steel industry managed to obtain protection from foreign competition, American automakers suddenly realized that steel cost them 40 percent more than it cost their foreign competitors. When the American semiconductor industry obtained protective clauses, the rest of the American computer industry was threatened with losing its competitive edge in relation to foreign manufacturers. When the American textile industry obtained a protected status, the entire American clothing industry suffered.

This new intertwining of all production with components from all over the world now makes it practically impossible to define the borders between various markets, barring a radical decision to establish overall protectionism. In a static world, in which the range of products and innovations is practically frozen, protectionism is an option that is not necessarily very costly. But the essential aspect of globalization as it is operating today, and no doubt the reason rendering it irrevocable, is that it is occurring at the same time as the third industrial revolution. This new revolution is producing a great decentralization of activities, thus stimulating the search for specific comparative advantages.

These considerations allow us to understand the growing difference between the protectionism of today and that of yesterday. The first industrial revolution, whose consequences were felt throughout the nineteenth century, is actually relatively easy to imitate. Paul Bairoch gives a humorous account of Marc Seguin's buying one locomotive, which he set up in the center of his workshop and had his employees copy.[11] If France decided today to copy innovations belonging to others (as India has attempted to do), all the while staying outside the system, it would quickly find itself banished by other countries, and it would lose the benefit of the continuous acceleration of new technologies. From this perspective, we might say that globalization has by now become inevitable.

Notes

Introduction

1. As quoted by Claude Nicolet in *Rendre à César* (Gallimard).

2. "The time has surely come to turn on its head that hoary and misleading explanation, still sometimes encountered, that it was the Turkish conquest which stimulated the great discoveries, whereas the reverse in fact occurred, for the great discoveries robbed the Levant of much of its appeal, enabling the Turks to extend their influence and settle there without too much difficulty." —Fernand Braudel, *The Mediterranean and the Mediterranean World in the Age of Philip II*, volume 2 (Harper & Row, 1973), pp. 666–667.

Chapter 1

1. Jean-Christophe Ruffin, *L'Empire et les Nouveaux Barbares* (Lattes, 1991).

2. Henri Mendras, *The Vanishing Peasant: Innovation and Change in French Agriculture* (MIT Press, 1970).

3. See René Dumont, *Démocratie pour l'Afrique* (Le Seuil, 1991).

4. See Robert Bates, *Towards a Political Economy of Development* (University of California Press, 1988).

5. Feudal armies in the Middle Ages were composed of knights in armor whose military might was on loan to their suzerain for a maximum period of forty days each year. By contrast, modern states as they have existed since the Renaissance have all attempted to establish

regular armies that can fight any day of the year—hence the unavoidable drain on royal finances.

6. As quoted by Dumont in *Démocratie pour l'Afrique.*

7. As quoted in P. Lane and A. Tornell, "Power, growth, and the voracity effect," *Journal of Economic Growth* 1 (June 1996): 213–241, which is also the source of the following examples.

8. One is Trinidad and Tobago, a country that benefited from its oil resources but then became poor over the period 1970–1990.

9. Not that they are entirely analogous; if such were the case, each country would be obliged to follow in the exact footsteps of the West in order to reach similar material prosperity.

Chapter 2

1. Paul Bairoch, *Mythes et paradoxes de l'histoire économique* (La Découverte, 1994).

2. My analysis is based on two brilliant articles by Alwyn Young: "A tale of two cities," in *NBER Macroeconomics Annual 1992*, and "The tyranny of numbers: Confronting the statistical realities of the East Asian growth experience," *Quarterly Journal of Economics* 110 (1995): 641–680. I also make use of Young's unpublished results on China, for which I thank him.

3. As late as 1974, more than 75 percent of the population had never received any education.

4. History will not easily forget that the bankruptcy of the Barings Bank (one of Britain's oldest financial institutions) originated in Singapore.

5. See Paul Romer, "Ideas determining convergence clubs," in Proceedings of the World Bank Annual Conference on Development Economics, 1992.

6. Paul Krugman, *Pop Internationalism* (MIT Press, 1996).

7. Alwyn Young, oral contribution, Seminar of International Monetary Economics, Paris.

8. Louis Dumont, *Homo aequalis* (Gallimard, 1976).

Chapter 3

1. James Goldsmith, *The Trap* (Carroll & Graf, 1993), pp. 26–27.

2. David Hume, *Essays, Moral, Political and Literary* (Oxford University Press, 1963).

3. See the introduction above.

4. See Nicolet, *Rendre à César*; see also Paul Veyne, *La société romaine* (Le Seuil, 1991).

5. William Petty, *Essays on Mankind and Political Arithmetic* (first edition: 1676).

6. Jean Fourastié, *Le grand espoir du XXème siècle* (Presses Universitaires de France, 1958).

7. The following is based on Paul Bairoch's book *Le tiers monde dans l'impasse* (Gallimard, 1983).

8. Gaston de Bernis, *Economie International* (Dalloz, 1976).

9. Neo-Ricardian theory as developed by Heckscher, Ohlin, and Samuelson is presented in all textbooks on international trade. See for example Paul Krugman and Maurice Obstfeld, *International Economics: Theory and Policy* (Scott, Foresman, 1988).

10. In general, despite the growing internationalization of financial markets, the role of capital in "globalization" actually remains very limited at present. We are very far from the time when Great Britain invested nearly half of its savings in foreign countries. Today, barely 1 to 2 percent of the capital of rich countries is invested in the South. These figures represent less than 10 percent of capital accumulation in poor countries themselves. Even if we leave out the 1980s (a decade during which the debt crisis forced poor countries to finance rich countries), the role of capital is far too modest to explain the polarization of the world.

11. Robert Reich, *The Work of Nations* (Knopf, 1991).

12. See Paul Romer, "Capital accumulation in the theory of long-run growth," in *Modern Business Cycle Theory*, ed. R. Barro (Harvard University Press, 1989); Gene Grossman and Elhanan Helpman, *Innovation and Growth in the Global Economy* (MIT Press, 1991).

13. A considerable number of studies have been devoted to this topic; most of them have concluded that trade accounts has a negligible effect on inequalities. See, for example, R. Lawrence and M. Slaughter,

"International trade and American wages in the 1980s: Giant sucking sound or small hiccup?" *Brookings Papers on Economic Activity (Microeconomics)* 2 (1993): 161–226; J. Sachs and H. Shatz, "Trade and jobs in US manufacturing," *Brookings Papers on Economic Activity* 1 (1994): 1–84. Adrian Wood reaches different conclusions in *North South Trade, Employment and Inequality: Changing Fortunes in a Skill Driven World* (Clarendon, 1994). Like other economists, Wood concludes that unweighted figures for trade cannot account for wage inequalities; however, his conclusion is based on the assumption that technological progress *in its entirety* is an endogenous response to trade with poor countries. Such an extreme hypothesis does not take into account the nature of contemporary technological progress—a point that will be developed in chapter 4 below.

14. See, for example, H. Bonnaz, N. Courtot, and D. Nivat, "Le contenu en emplois des échanges industriels de la France avec les pays en voie de développement," *Economie et Statistique* no. 279 (1994): 13–34.

Chapter 4

1. Source: Lester Thurow, *The Future of Capitalism* (Morrow, 1996). See also the February 1992 special issue of *Quarterly Journal of Economics*, which is devoted to wage disparities.

2. Jeffrey Williamson and Peter Lindert, *American Inequality: A Macroeconomic History* (Academic Press, 1980).

3. C. Goldin and R. Margo "The Great Compression: The wage structure in the United States at mid-century," *Quarterly Journal of Economics* 107 (February 1992)" 1–34.

4. We all know how unsatisfactory this categorization is.

5. Fast-food jobs are considered by the French to be the hidden face of pseudo-full-time employment in the US.

6. Dominique Goux and Eric Maurin, La transformation de la demande de travail par qualification en France (working paper, INSEE, 1995).

7. See, for example, G. Borjas, R. Freeman, and L. Katz, *On the Labor Market Effects of Immigration and Trade* (University of Chicago Press, 1992); L. Katz and K. Murphy, "Changes in relative

wages, 1963–1987: Supply and demand factors," *Quarterly Journal of Economics* 107 (February 1992): 35–78.

8. Goux and Maurin "La transformation de la demande de travail par qualification en France."

9. Michael Kremer, "The O-Ring theory of economic development," *Quarterly Journal of Economics* 108 (August 1993): 551–575.

10. As measured by wage differentials within a firm. See Francis Kramarz, Stefan Lollivier, and Louis-Paul Pele, Wage inequalities and firm-specific compensation in France (working paper, INSEE, 1994).

11. After doubts were cast on the quality of his work, Jacques Dorfman, once reputed to be the best of France's tennis umpires, went from umpiring at Roland-Garros to judging beach tournaments. No negotiation of his salary could have stopped his decline as soon as the doubts set in.

12. Compaq and Hewlett-Packard are still all-American.

13. The "founding" essay of this school is Michel Aglietta's *Régulation et crises du capitalisme* (Calmann-Lévy, 1976). See also Robert Boyer, *La théorie de la régulation: une analyse critique* (La Découverte, 1987); Robert Boyer and Yves Saillard, *La régulation: l'état des savoirs* (La Découverte, 1996).

14. See Edward Behr, *L'Amérique qui fait peur* (Plon, 1995).

15. Robert Castel, *Les métamorphoses de la société salariale* (Fayard, 1994).

Chapter 5

1. This phrase is borrowed from the title of a book by Jean-Paul Fitoussi and Pierre Rosanvallon: *Le nouvel âge des inégalités* (Le Seuil, 1996).

2. See two MIT working papers: Michael Kremer and Eric Maskin, Segregation by Skill and the Rise of Inequality (1996); Daron Acemoglu, Matching, Heterogeneity and the Evolution of Income (1995).

3. Agnès van Zanten, "Fabrication et effets de la ségrégation scolaire," in *L'exclusion: l'état des savoirs*, ed. S. Paugam (La Découverte, 1996).

4. Gary Becker, *A Treatise on the Family*, second edition (Harvard University Press, 1991). The concept of assortative matching is borrowed from Becker.

5. Along the same lines, the economist Douglas North accounts for the decline of feudalism by underlining the sudden scarcity of farmers after the Great Plague of the fourteenth century. North attributes the transformation of peasant life as well as the decline of feudal power to the relative abundance of land—a production factor which is complementary to the farmers. See Douglas North and Robert Thomas, *The Rise of the Western World* (Cambridge University Press, 1973).

6. François de Singly, *Le soi, le couple, la famille* (Nathan, 1996).

7. Norbert Elias, *The Civilising Process* (Blackwell, 1996; first edition published in 1939).

8. Louis Dumont, *Homo aequalis* (Gallimard, 1976).

9. Irène Théry, *Le démariage* (Odile Jacob, 1993).

10. Pascal Bruckner, *La mélancolie démocratique* (Le Seuil, 1990).

11. The common currency took a long time to achieve institutional status, as is the case in Europe today.

12. Alberto Alesina and Enrico Spaloare, The Size of Nations (working paper, Harvard University, 1995); Patrick Bolton and Gérard Roland, The Break-up of Nations (working paper, Université Libre de Bruxelles, 1995).

Chapter 6

1. Disparities in estate holdings are altogether different in nature: the rise in interest rates and the aging of the population have strongly exacerbated them. Likewise, the rise in income inequalities (which include more than wage inequalities) has been automatically increased by unemployment.

2. This idea is developed in my book *The Misfortunes of Prosperity* (MIT Press, 1995).

3. For an excellent survey, see Charlie Bean, "European unemployment," *Journal of Economic Literature* 32 (July 1994): 573–619.

4. On this important point, see C. Sorrentino, "International comparisons of unemployment indicators," *Monthly Labor Review*, [month] 1993: 3–19.

5. A. Michael Spence, *Market Signaling: Informational Transfer in Hiring and Related Screening Processes* (Harvard University Press, 1974).

6. Christian Baudelot and Michel Glaude, "Les salaires se dévaluent—ils en se multipliant?" *Economie et statistique* 225 (October 1989): 3–16.

7. The Phillips curve was introduced by A. W. H. Phillips in his article "The relation between unemployment and the rate of change of money-wage in the United Kingdom, 1861–1957," *Economica* 25 (1958): 283–299.

8. M. Bruno and J. Sachs, *Economics of Worldwide Stagflation* (Harvard University Press, 1985).

9. P. A. Muet, Chômage et politique économique (report 9406, Office Français des Conjonctures Economiques, 1994).

10. According to Muet, a one-point *rise* in unemployment statistically reduces wage inflation by 0.4 point. This means that the rise in unemployment during the 1980s accounts for ("causes") more than half the amount of disinflation.

11. Philippe d'Iribarne, *La logique de l'honneur* (Le Seuil, 1989).

12. See D. Cohen, A. Lefranc, and G. Saint-Paul, "French unemployment: A transatlantic perspective," *Economic Policy* 2 (1997): 265–292.

Chapter 7

1. See Jean Peyrelevade, Le poids du vieillissement (note, Fondation Saint-Simon, 1996).

2. Dominique Schnapper, "Intégration et exclusion dans les sociétés modernes," in *L'exclusion: l'état des savoirs*, ed. S. Paugam (La Découverte).

3. See Agnès Van Zanten's analysis, quoted in chapter 5.

4. Denis Fougère, "Trajectoires des chômeurs de longue durée," in *L'exclusion*, ed. Paugam.

5. See Milton Friedman, *Capitalism and Freedom* (University of Chicago Press). Friedman invented the formula. For France, see Lionel Stoleru, *Vaincre la pauvreté dans les pays riches* (Flammarion).

6. See Alain Caillé, *Critique de la raison utilitaire* (La Découverte, 1989).

7. For a possible application to France, see Thomas Piketty, La redistribution fiscale face au chômage (working paper, CEPREMAP, Paris, 1996).

8. This example is drawn from Raquel Fernandez and Dani Rodrik, "Resistance to reform: Status quo bias in the presence of individual-specific uncertainty," *American Economic Review* 81, no. 5 (1991): 1146–1155.

9. Pierre Rosanvallon, *La nouvelle question sociale: Repenser l'Etat-Providence* (Le Seuil, 1995).

10. Thomas Piketty, "Social mobility and redistributive politics," *Quarterly Journal of Economics* 110, no. 3 (1995): 551–584.

11. This experiment was conducted by Boaz Weinstein. See his working paper Effects of Expected and Unexpected Rewards on Altruism in Children (Midwood High School, Brooklyn, N.Y., 1995).

Epilogue

1. See, for example, R. Barro and X. Sala-i-Martin, *Economic Growth* (McGraw-Hill, 1995).

2. Paul Romer, "Capital accumulation in the theory of long-run growth," in *Modern Business Cycle Theory* (Harvard University Press, 1989).

3. Jacques Cauvin, *Naissance des dieux, naissance de l'agriculture* (CNRS, 1994).

4. Ibid.

5. Ibid.

6. Ibid.

7. Braudel, in *Grammaire des Civilisations* (Arthaud-Flammarion, 1987), as quoted by Jean-François Bayart in *La ré-invention du capitalisme* (Karthala, 1994). The latter volume contains many concrete illustrations of Braudel's point.

8. Jean Fourastié, *Le grand esprit du xx siècle* (Presses Universitaires de France, 1958).

9. Paul Bairoch, *Le tiers-monde dans l'impasse* (Gallimard, 1983).

10. Reich, *The Work of Nations*.

11. Bairoch, *Le tiers-monde dans l'impasse*.

Index